Copyright© 2020

All rights reserved.
No part of this publication
may be reproduced,
distributed or transmitted
in any form or by any means
including photocopying,
recording or other
electronic or mechanical
methods without
the prior written
permission of the publisher
except in the case
of brief quotations
embodied in critical reviews
and certain other
non commercial uses permitted
by copyright law.

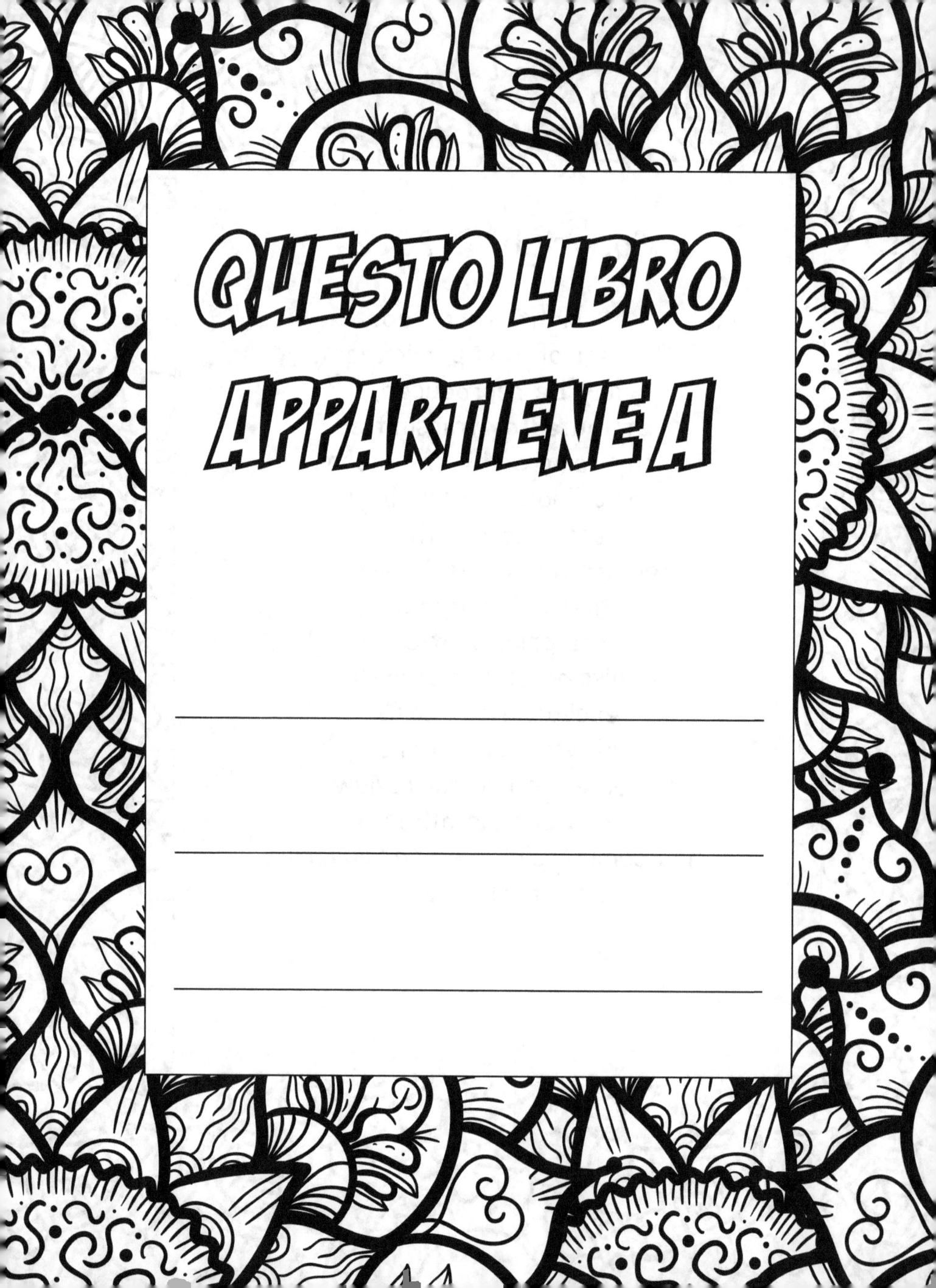

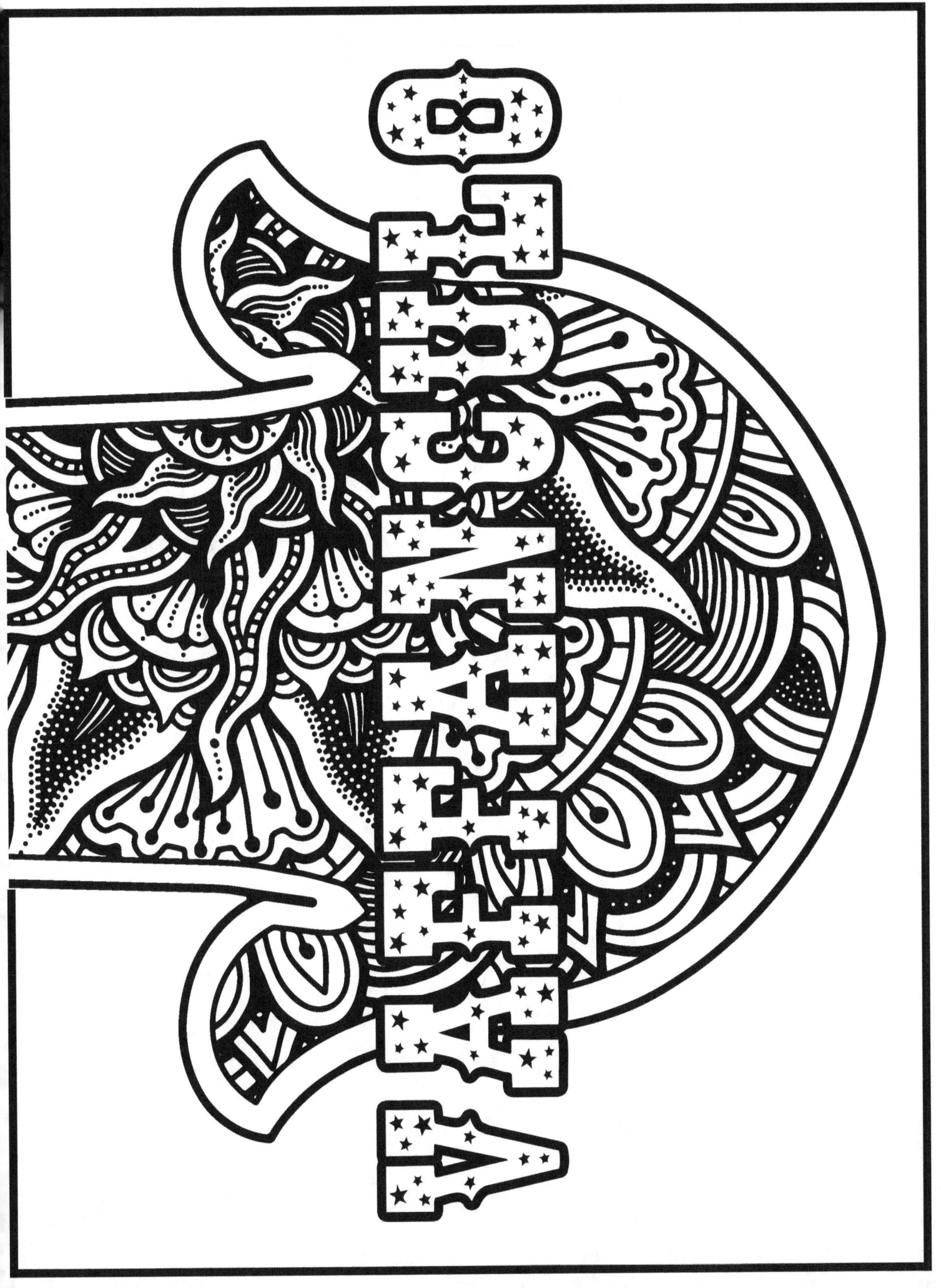

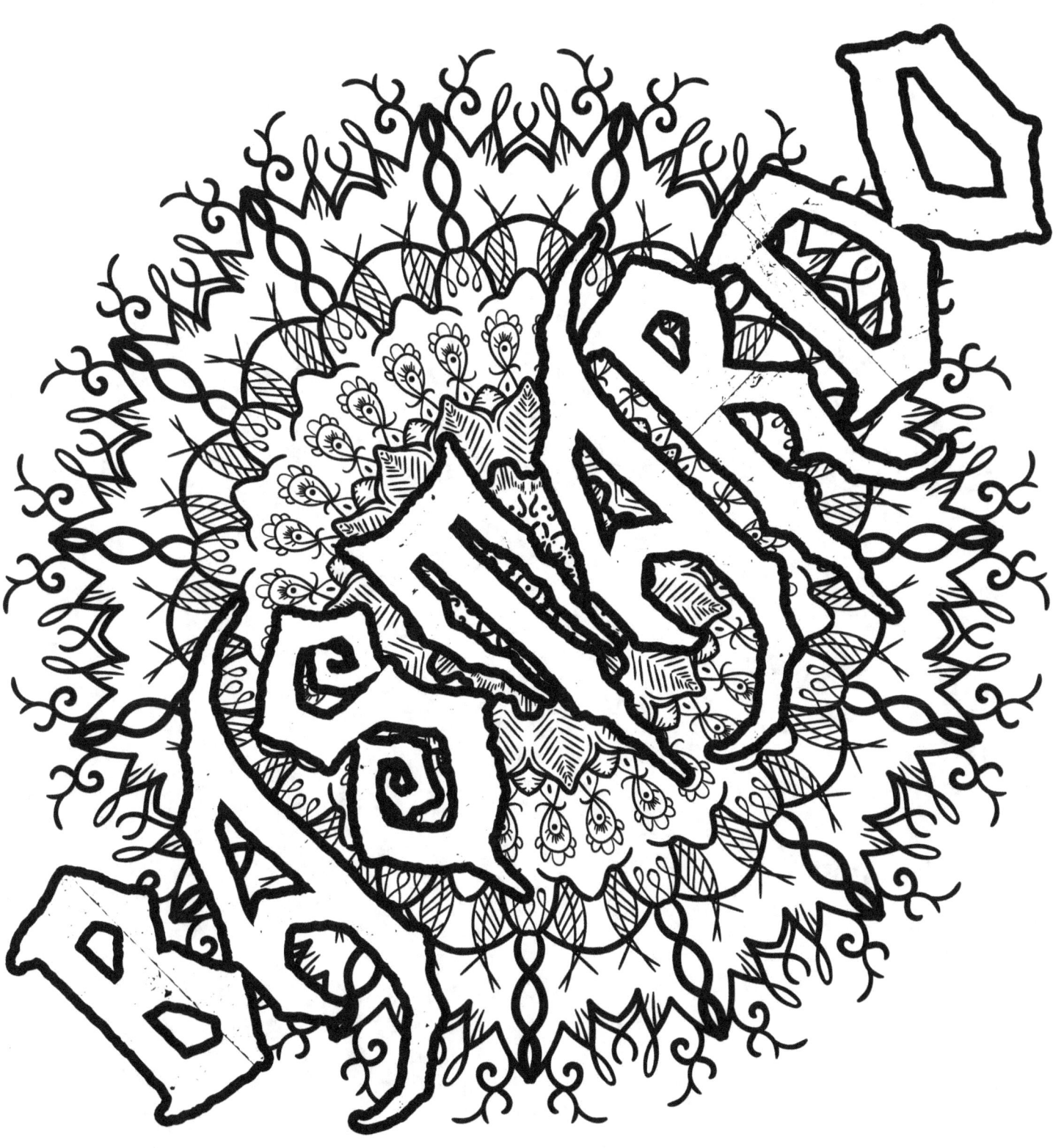

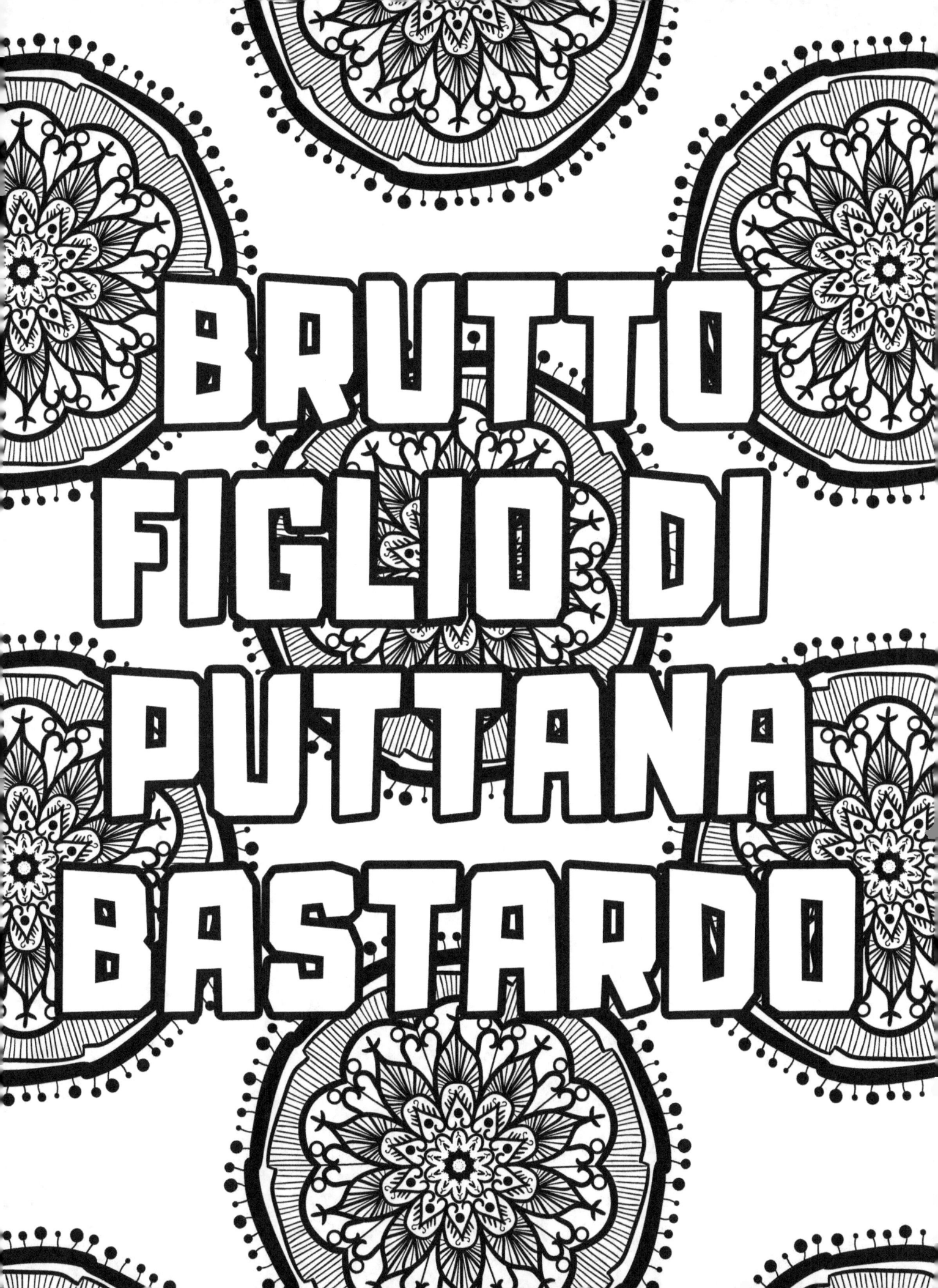

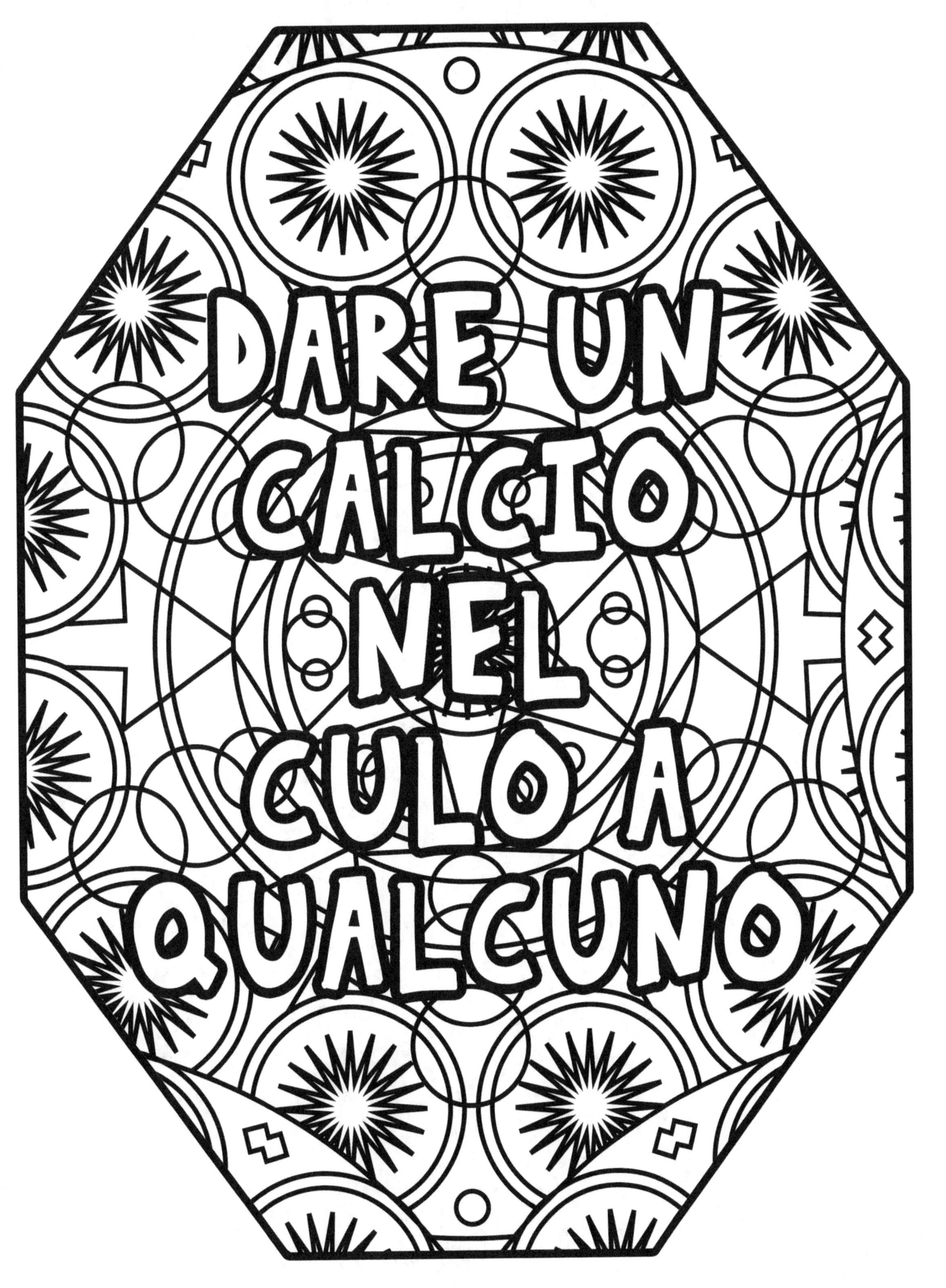

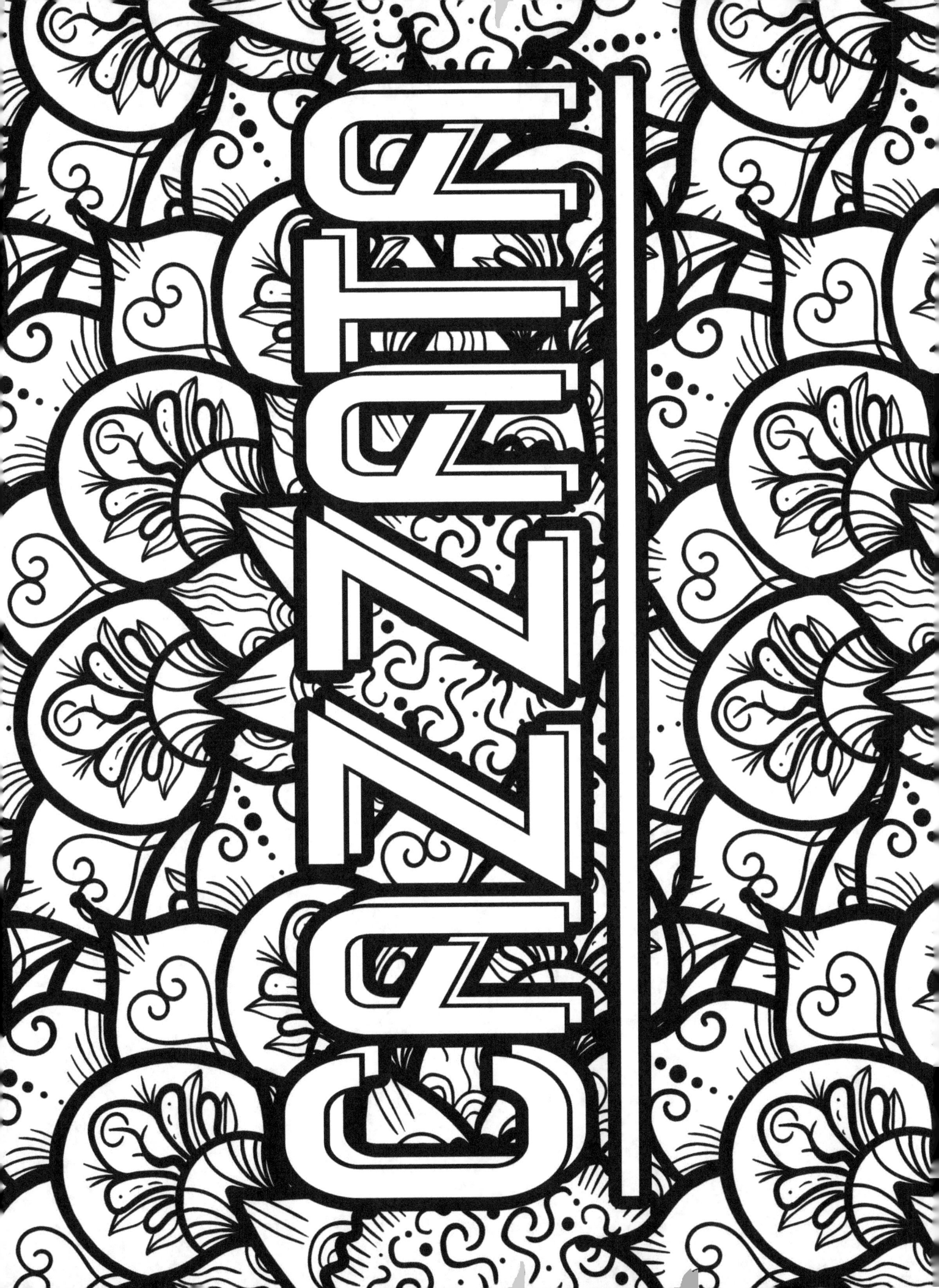

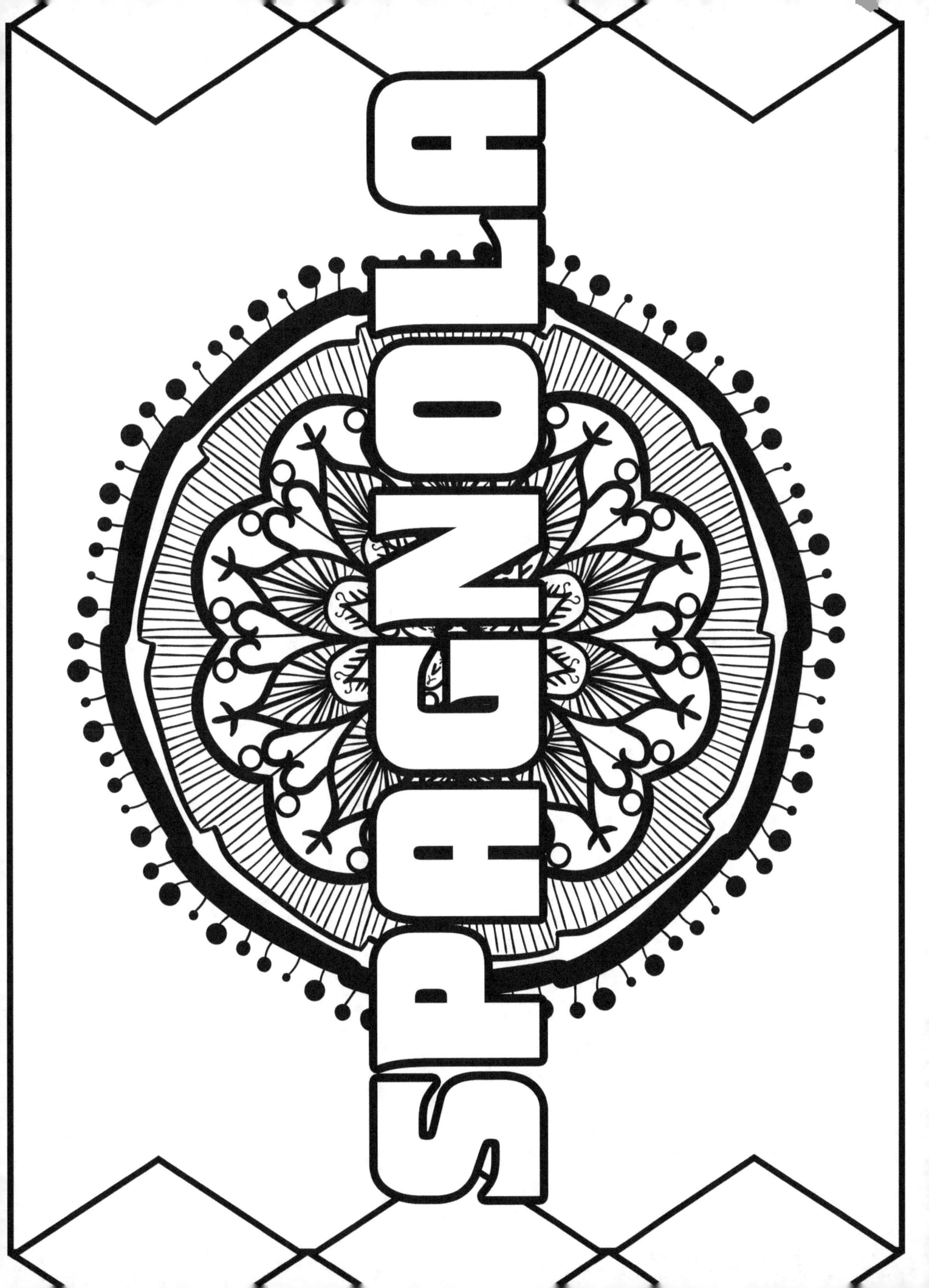

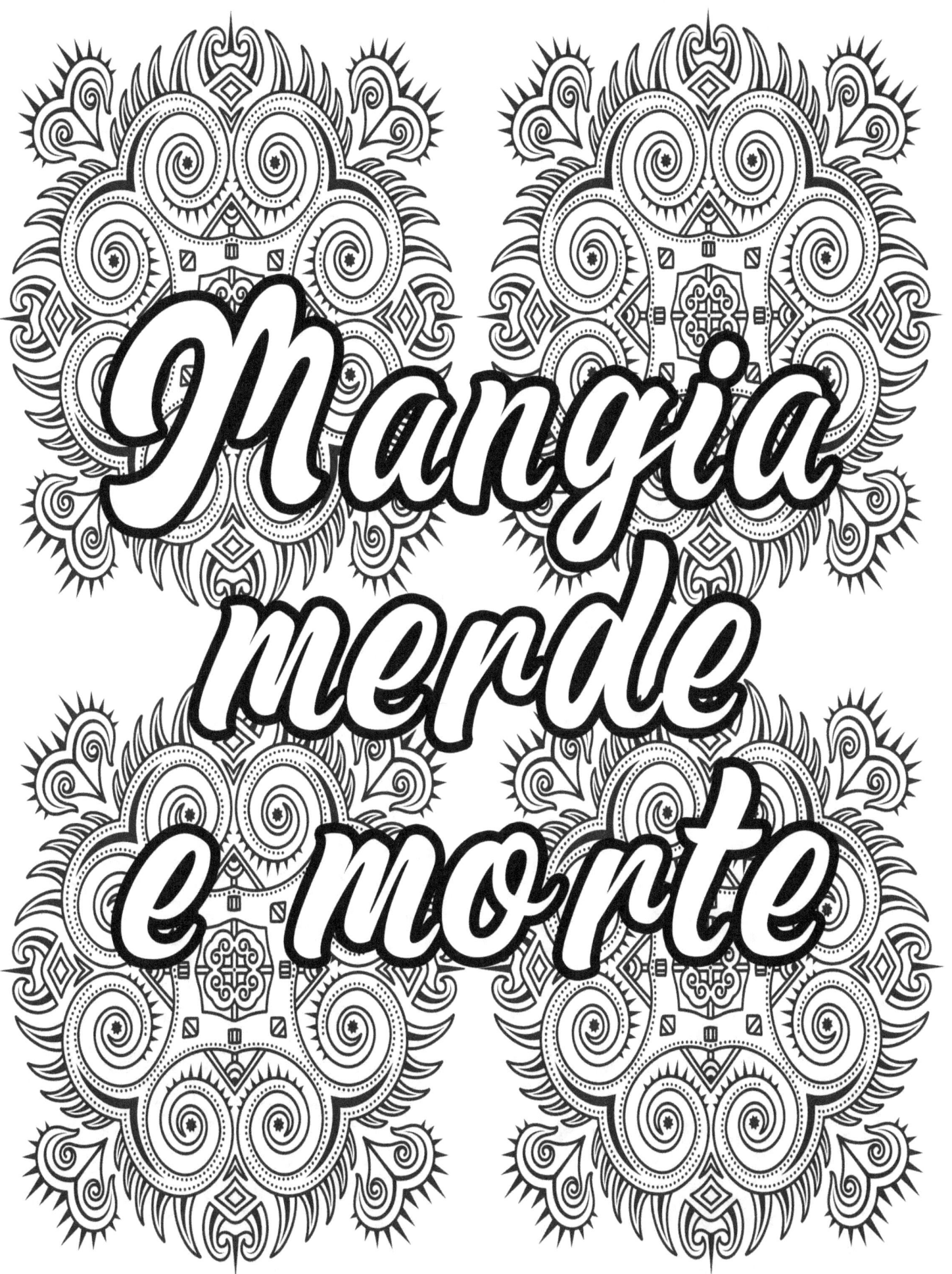

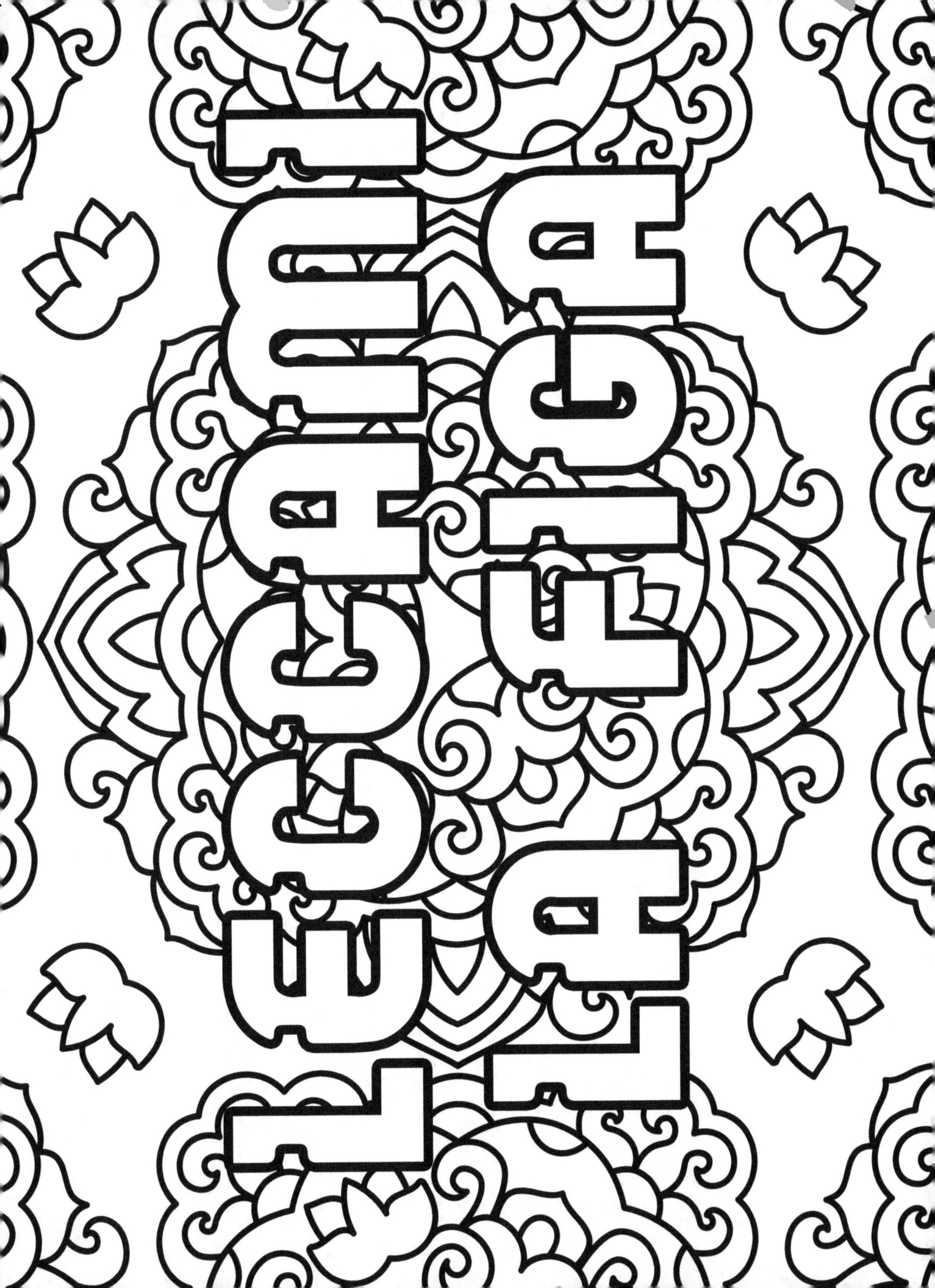

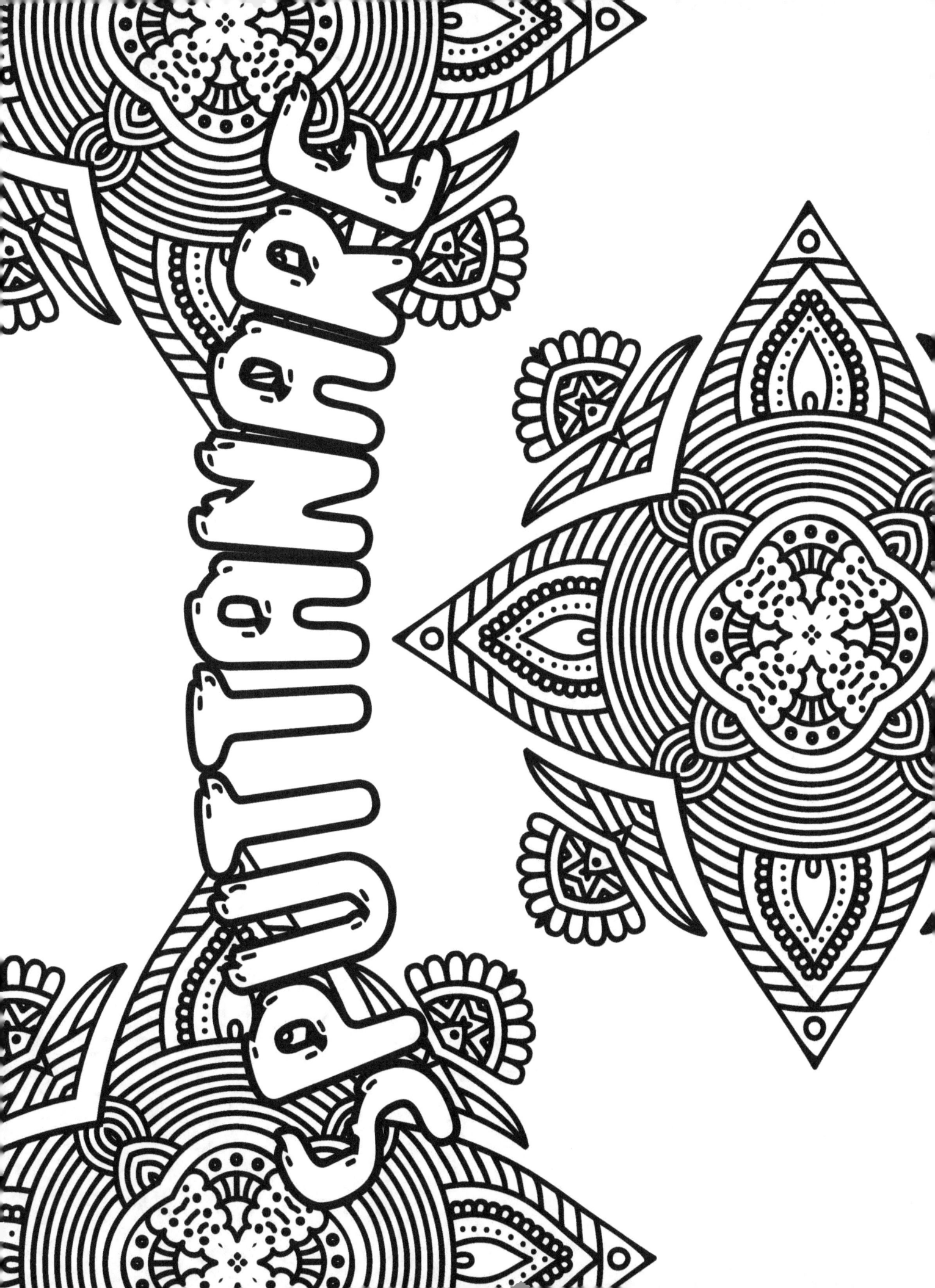

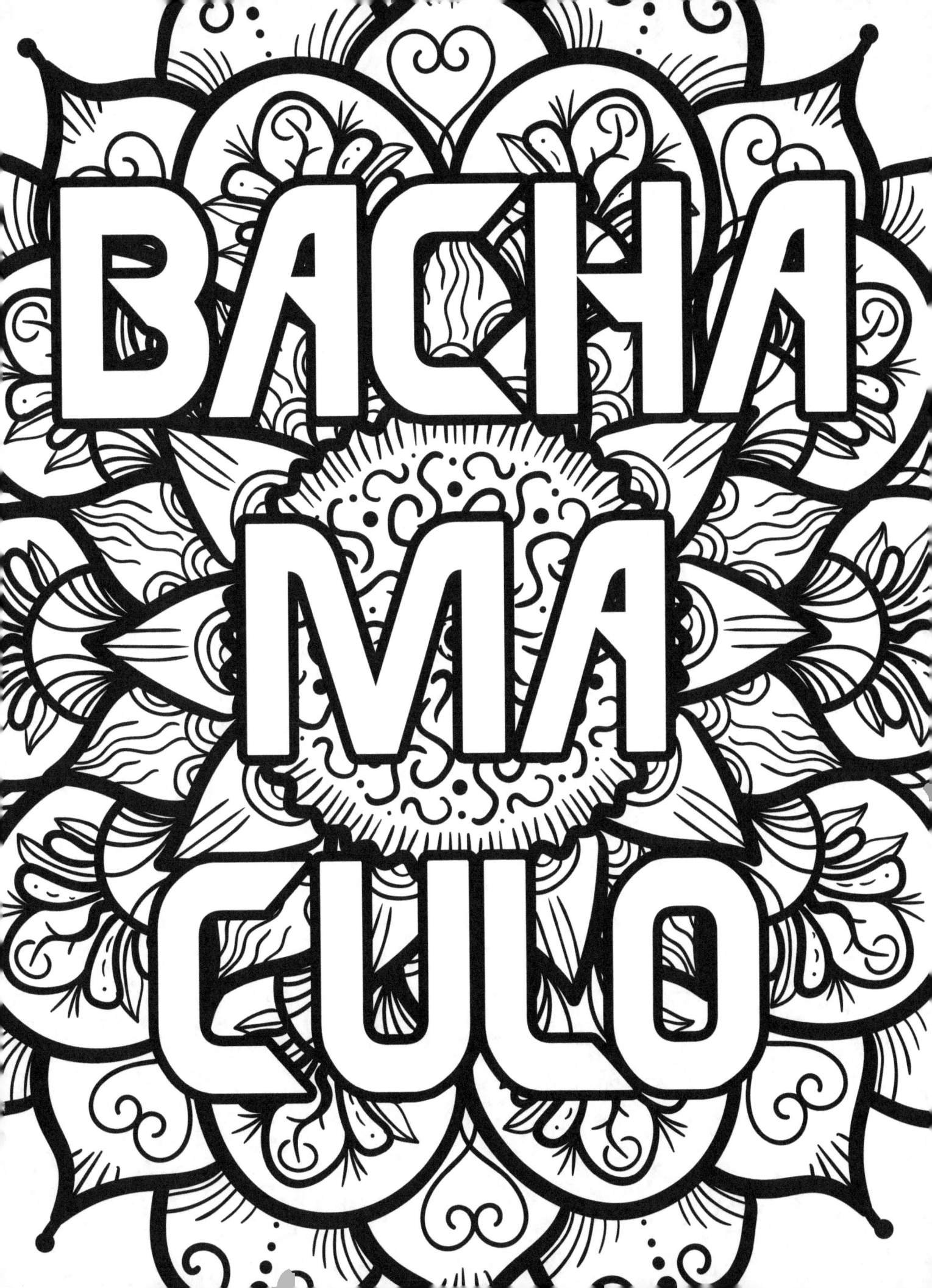

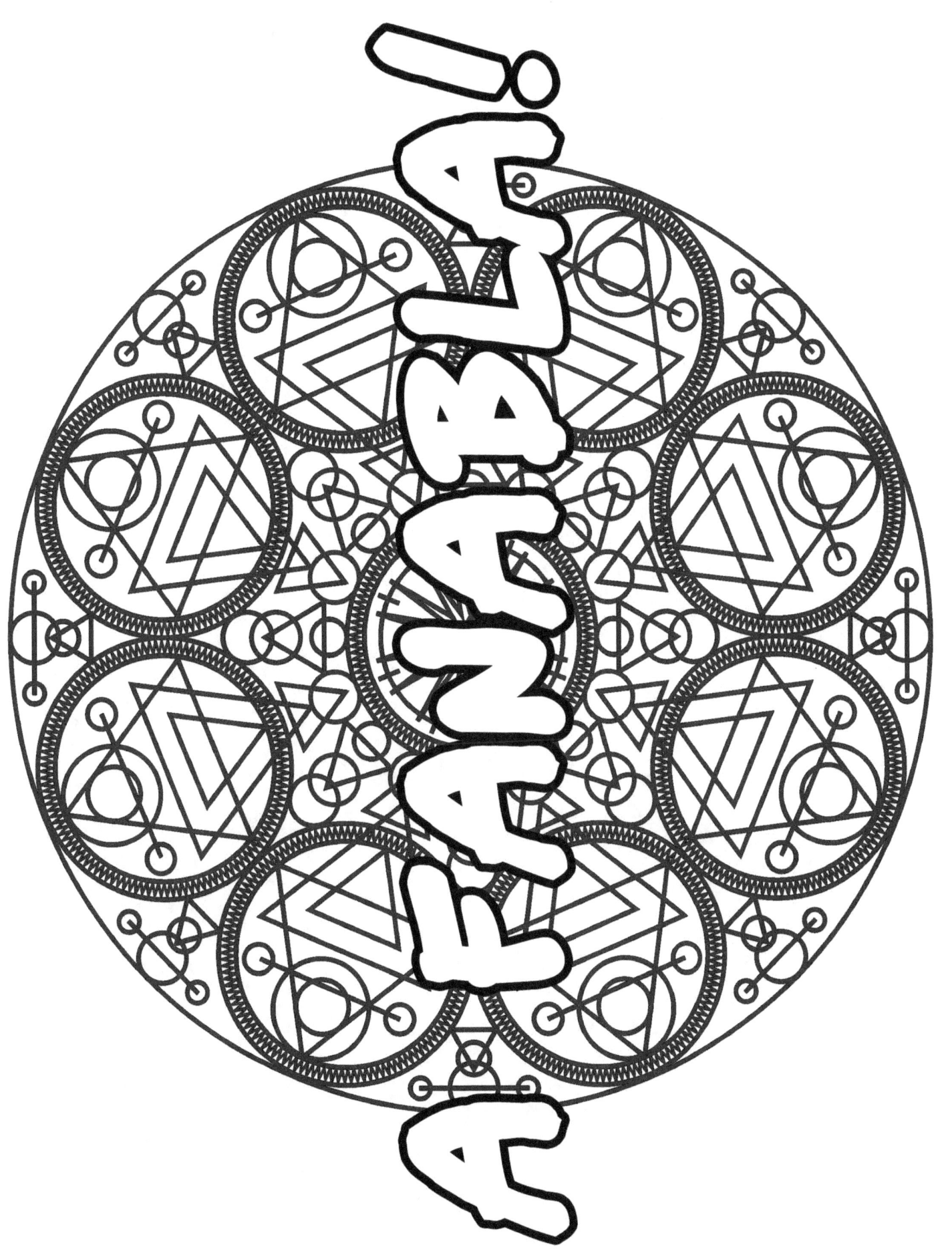

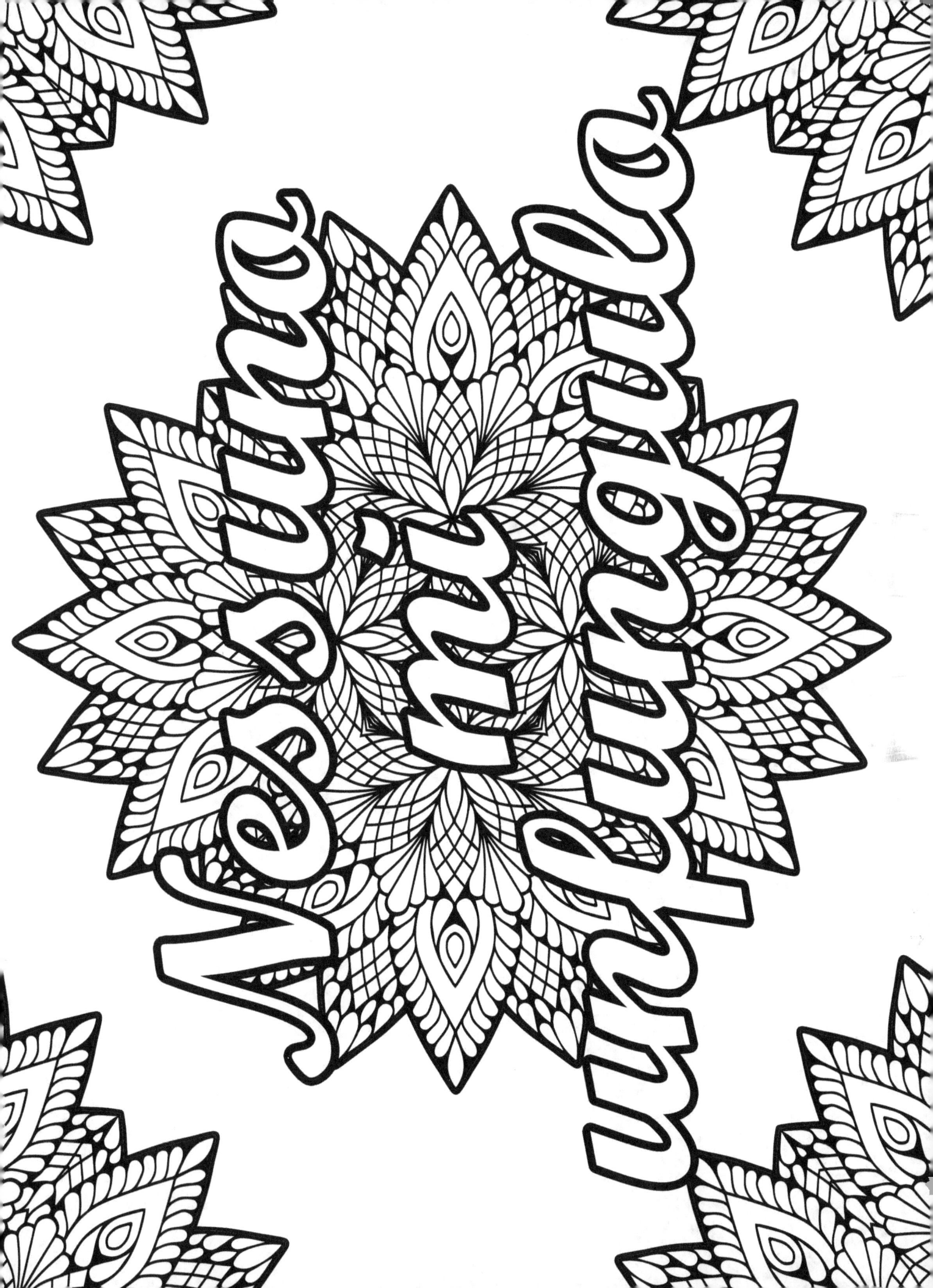

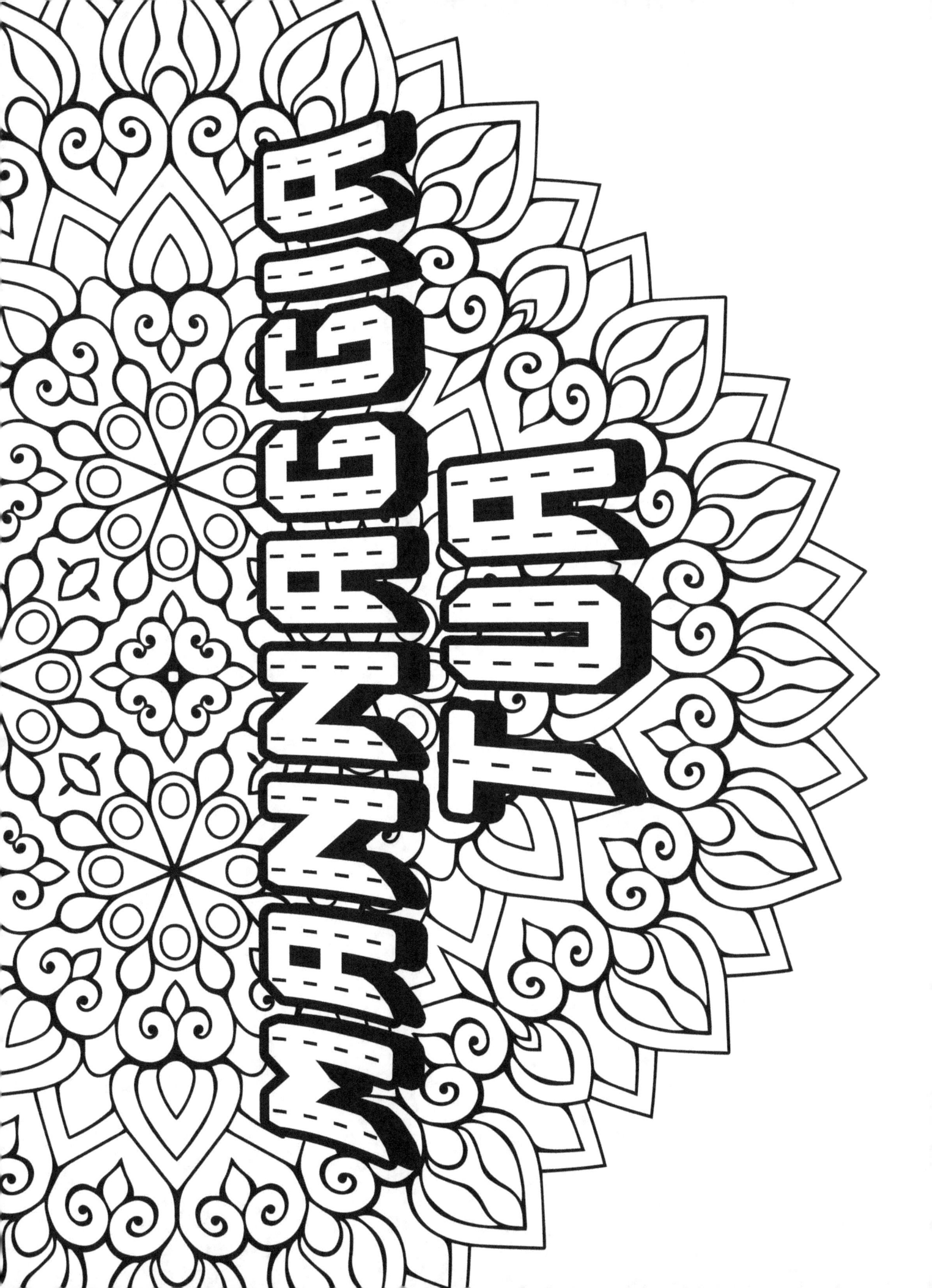

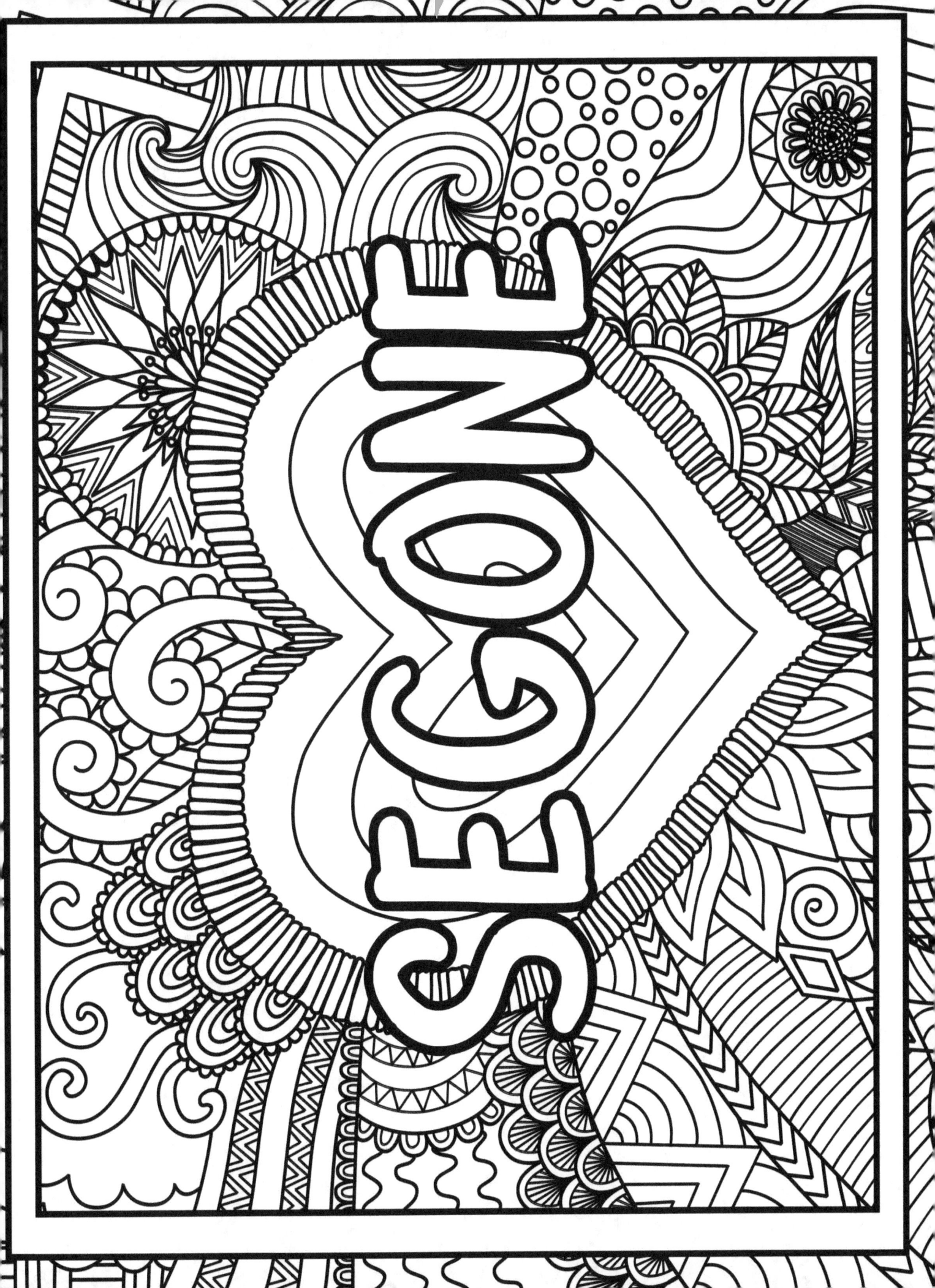

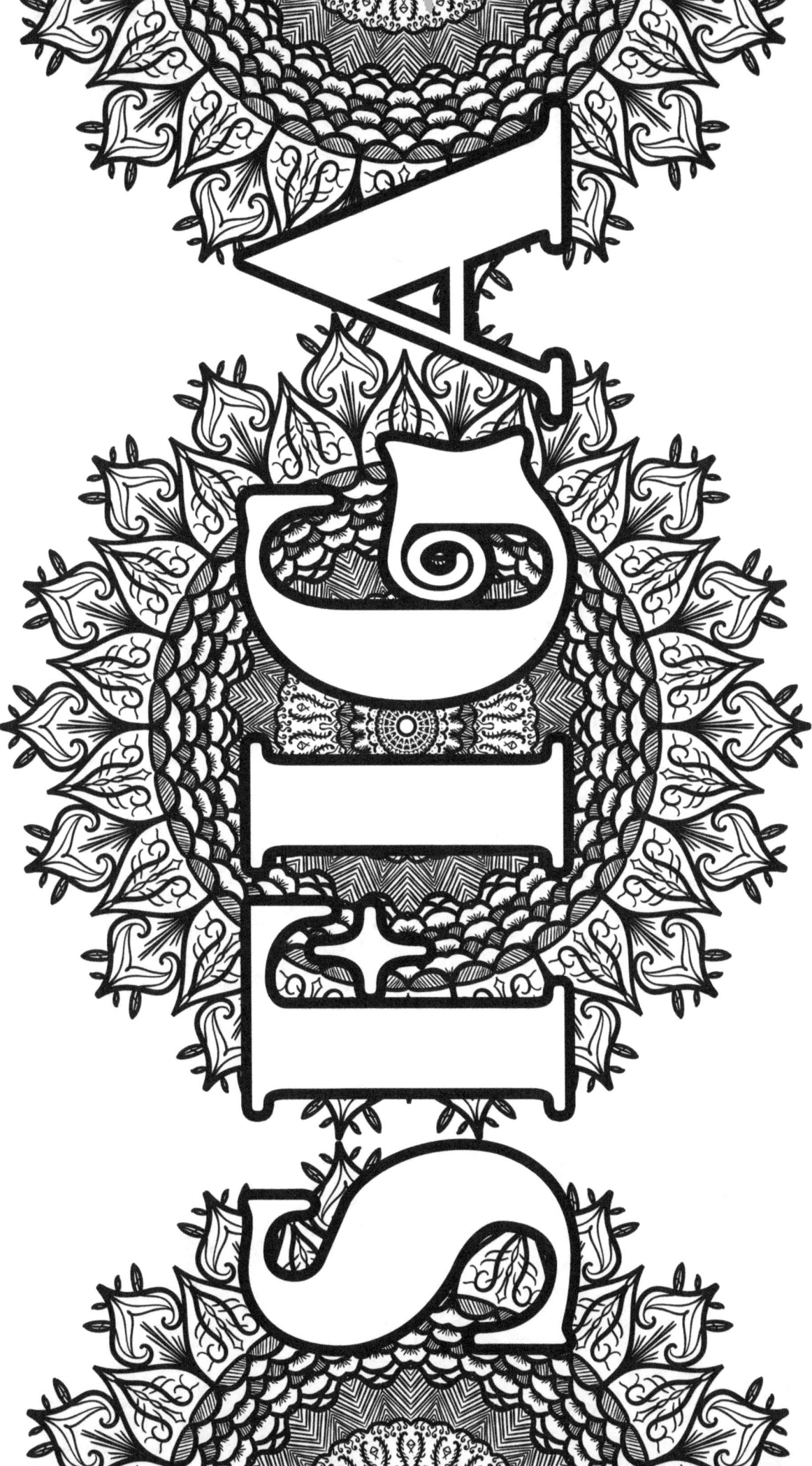

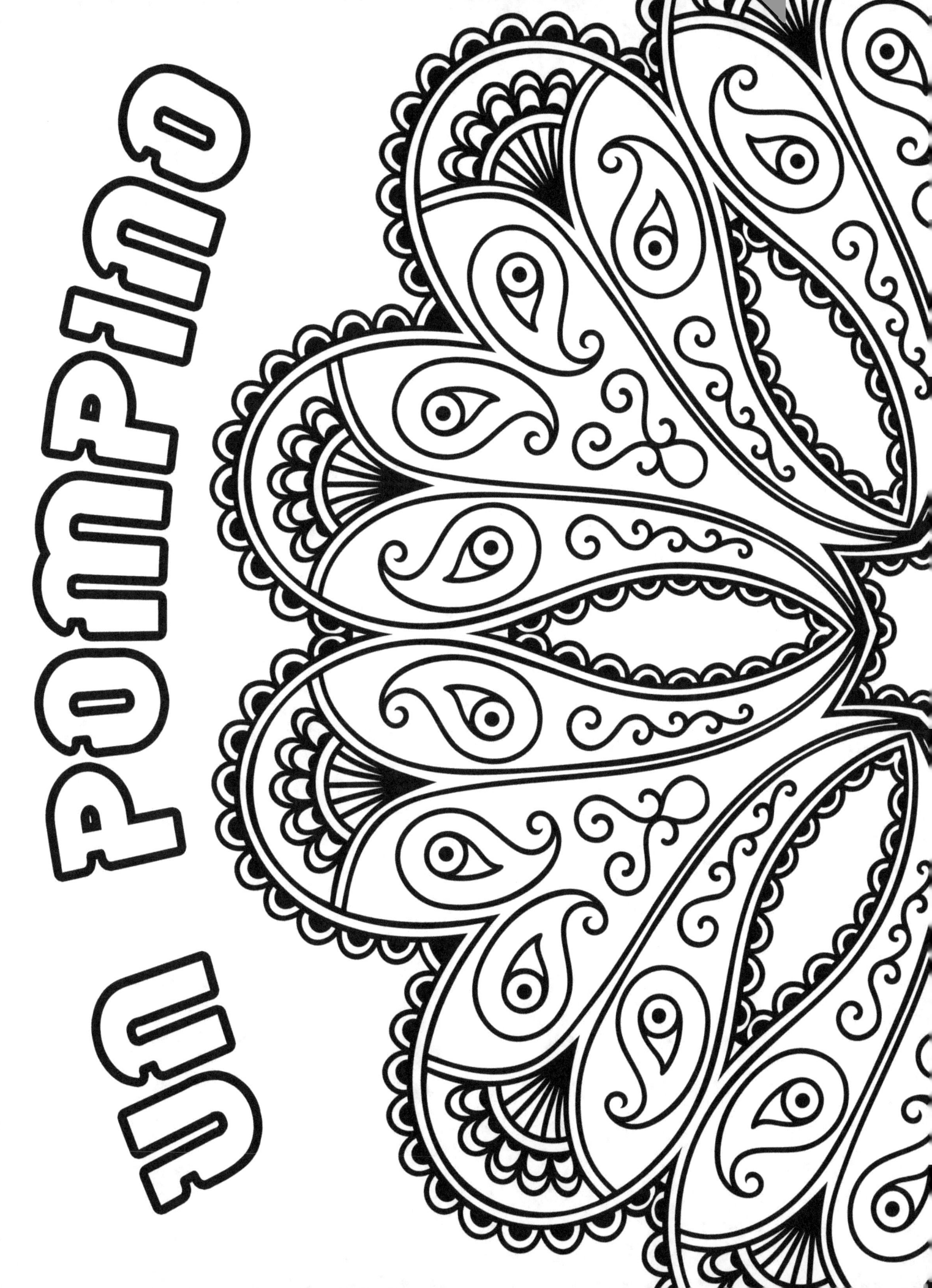

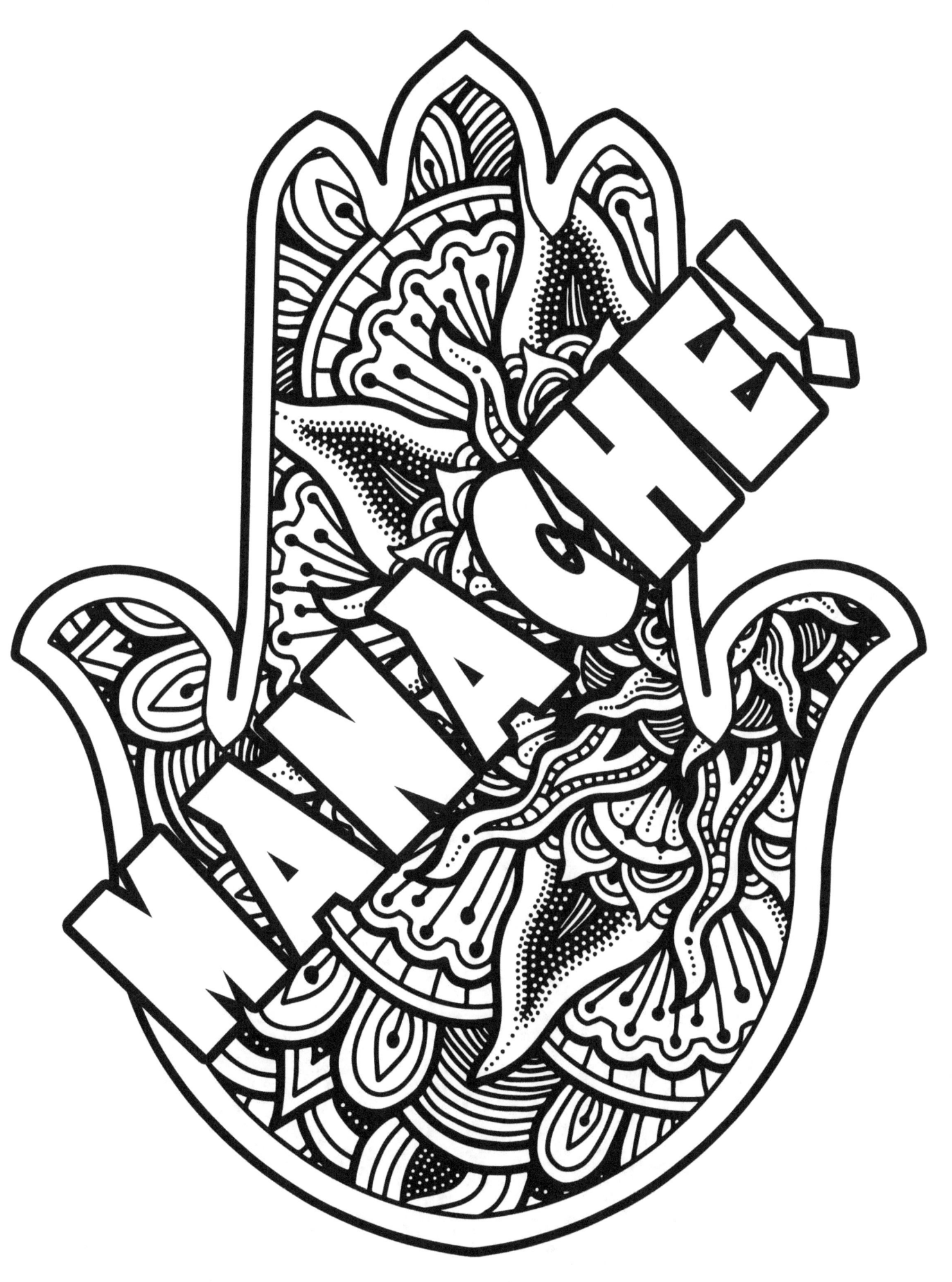

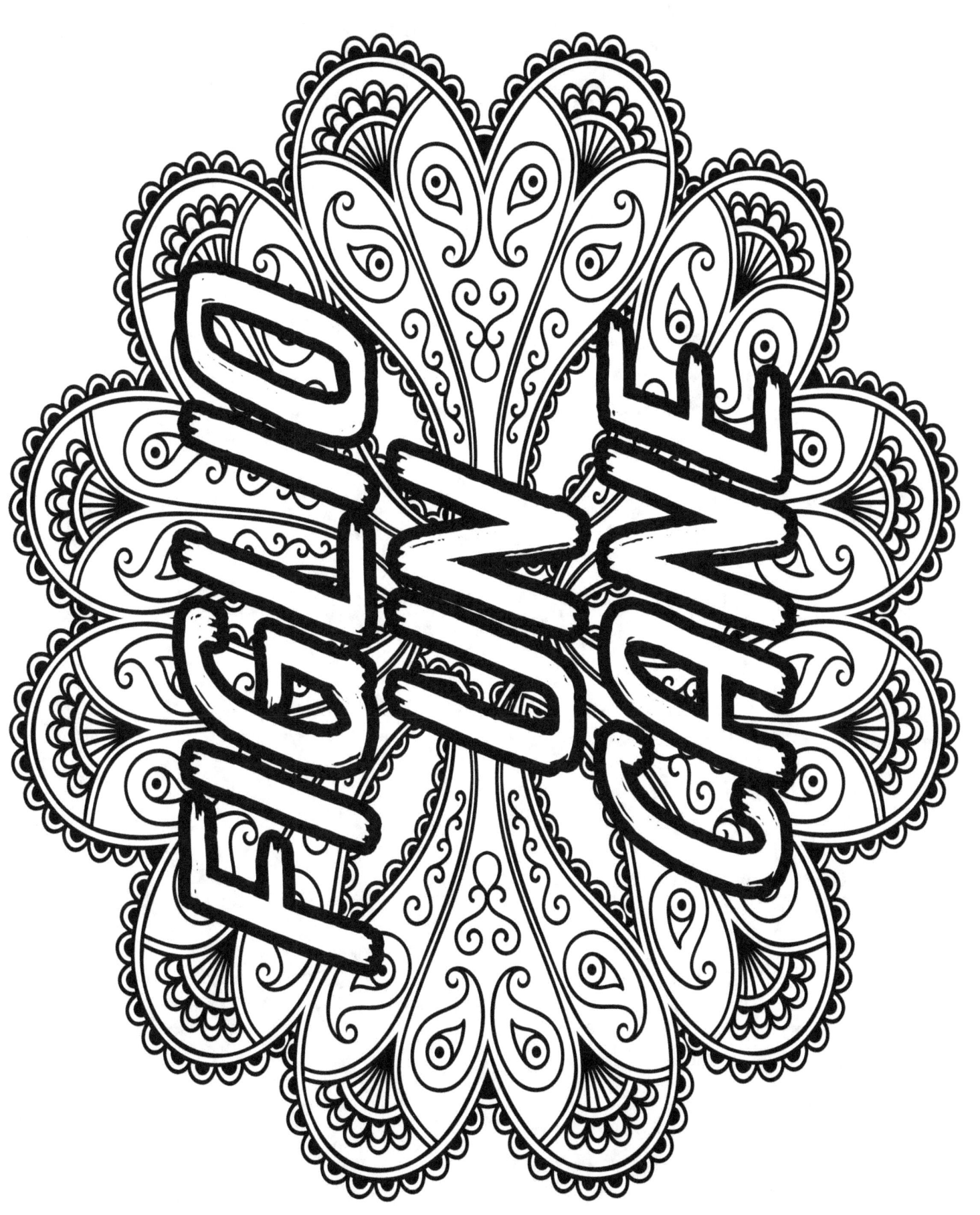

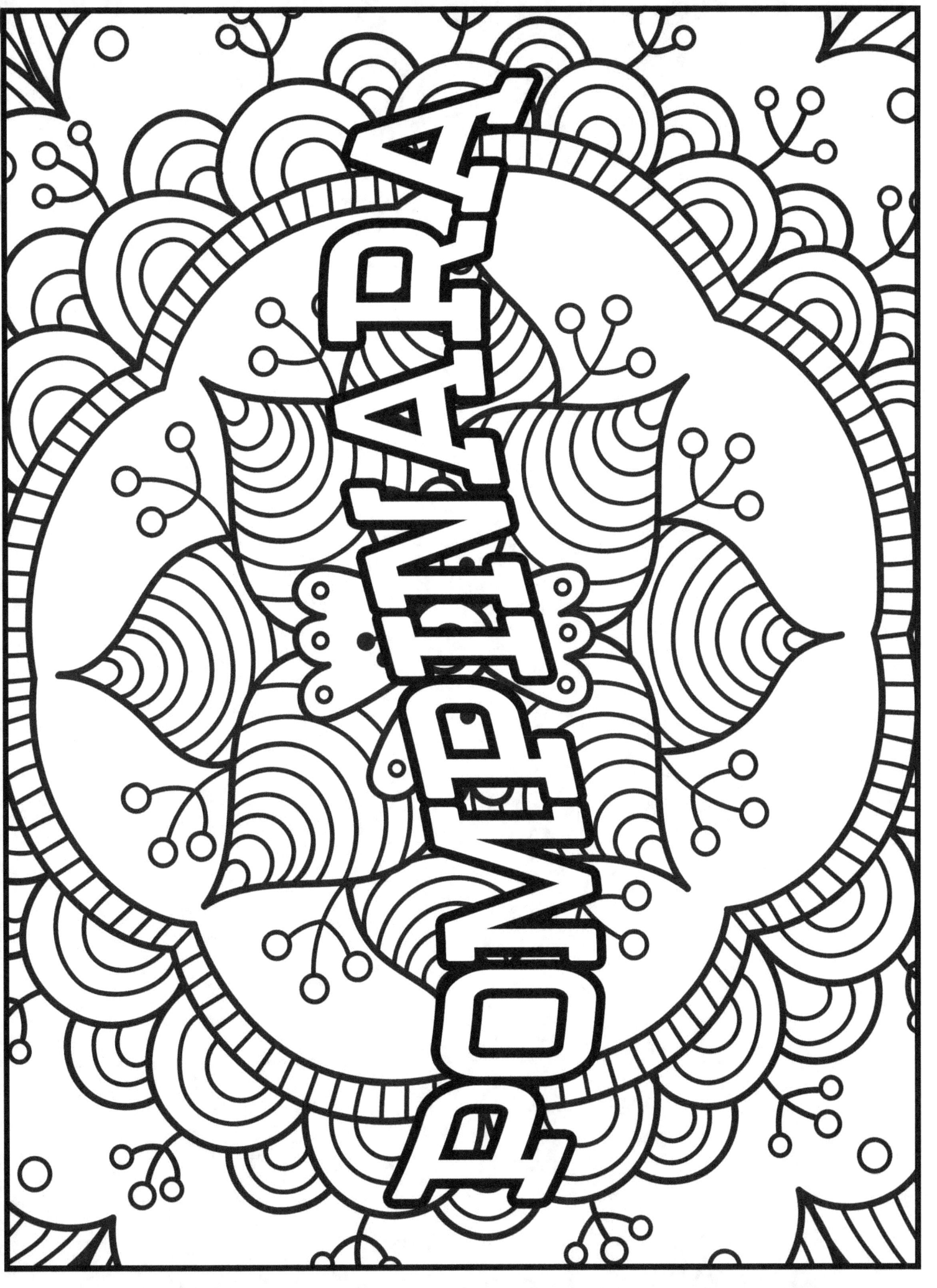

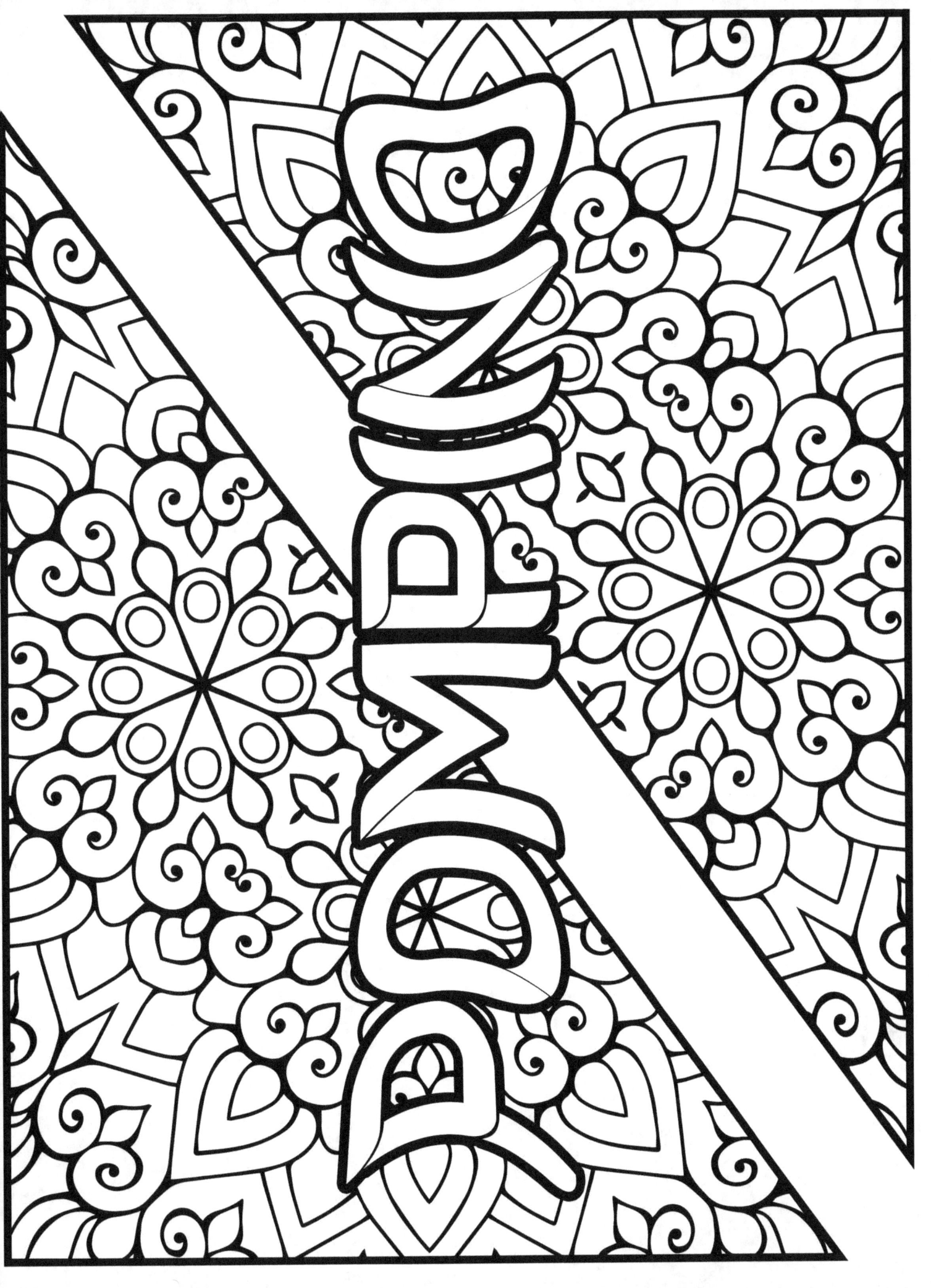

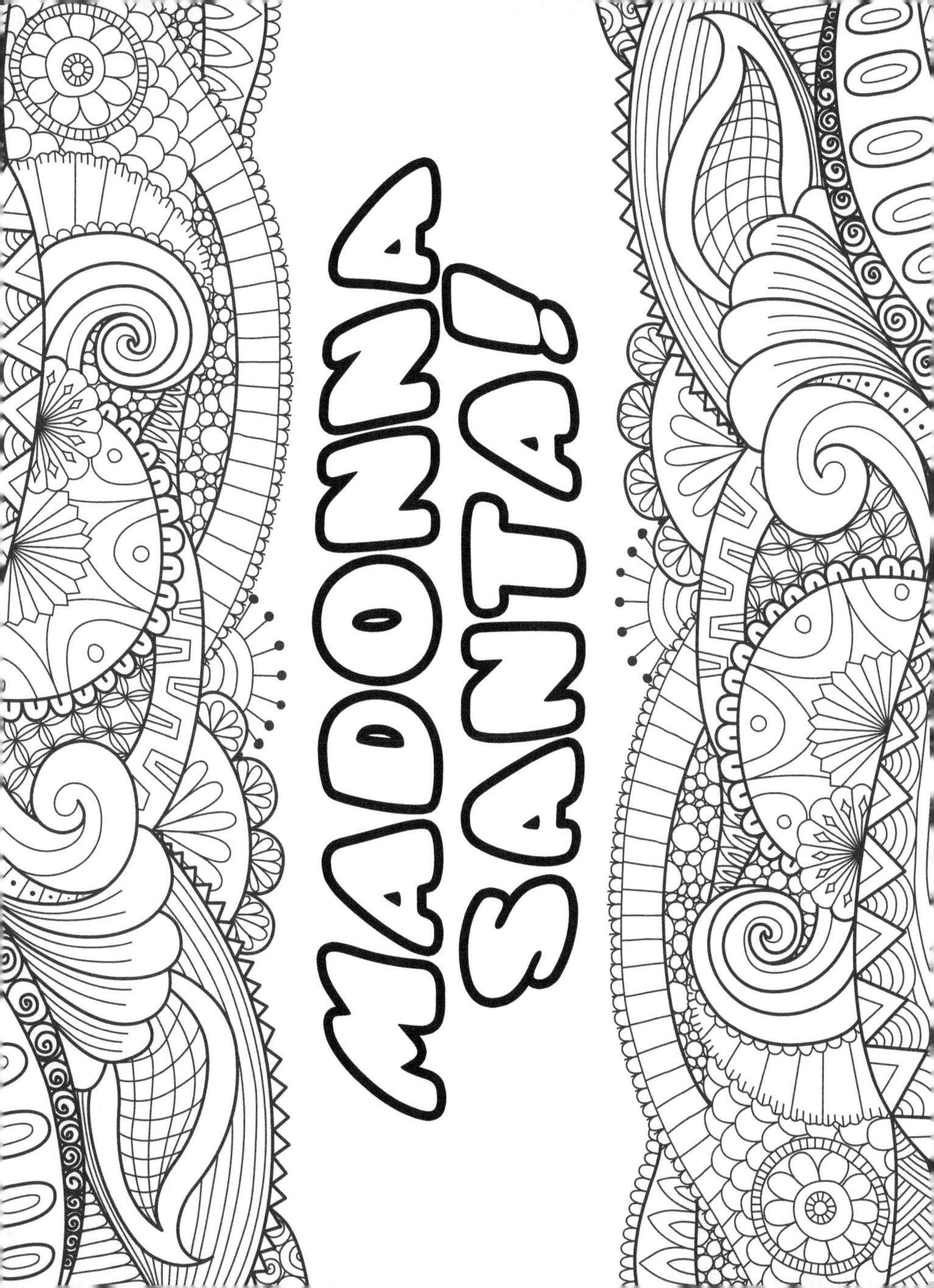

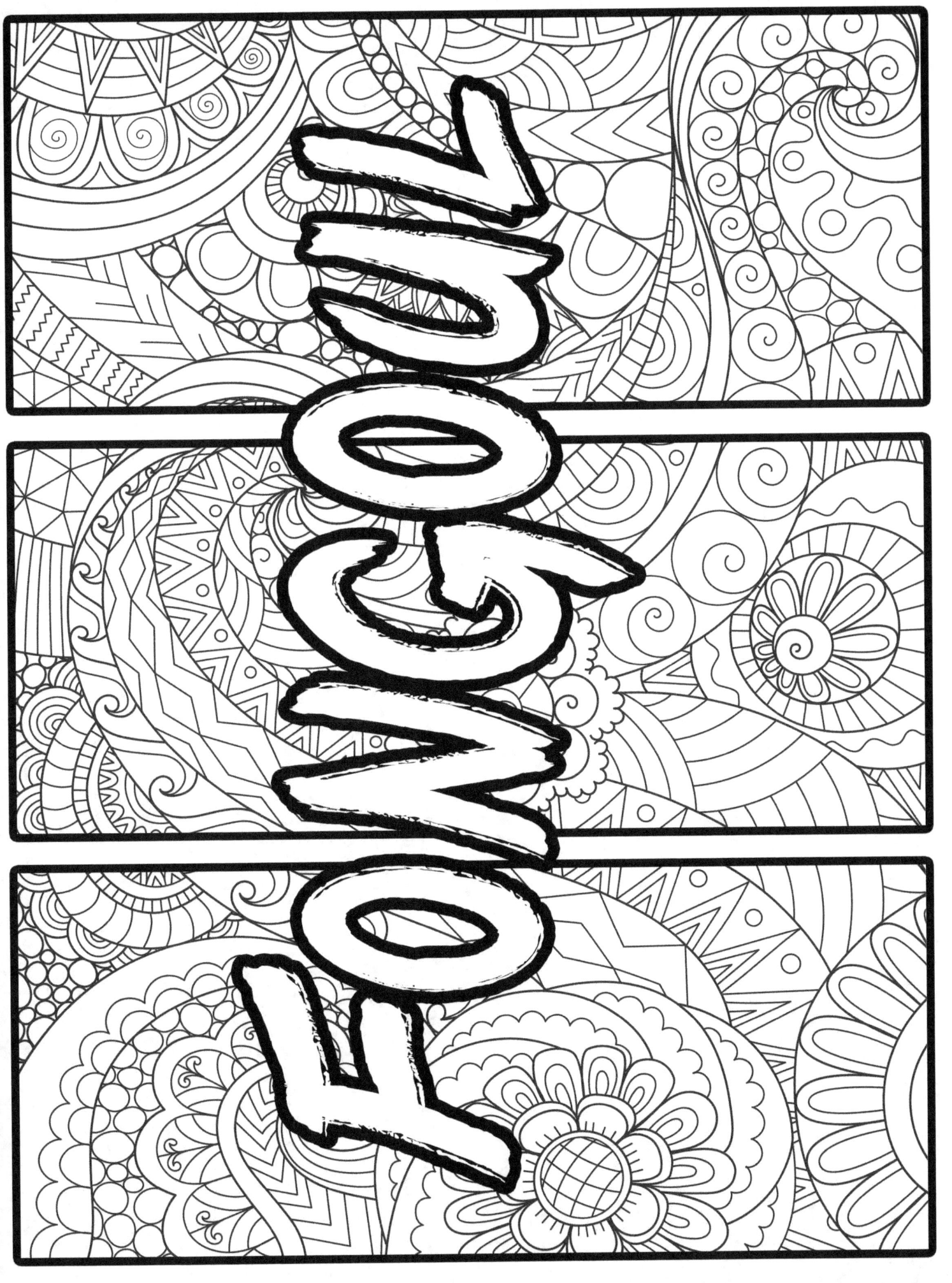

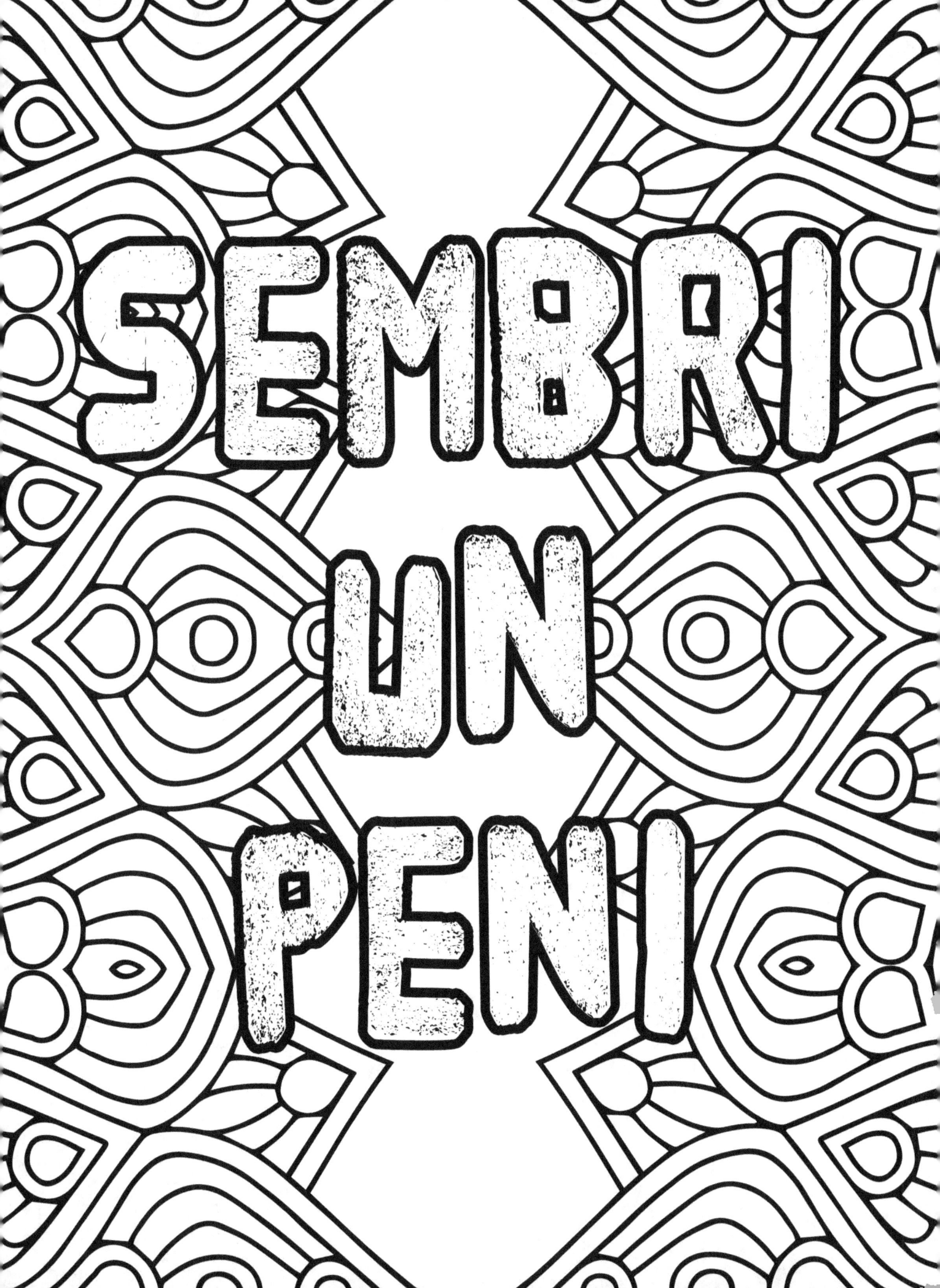

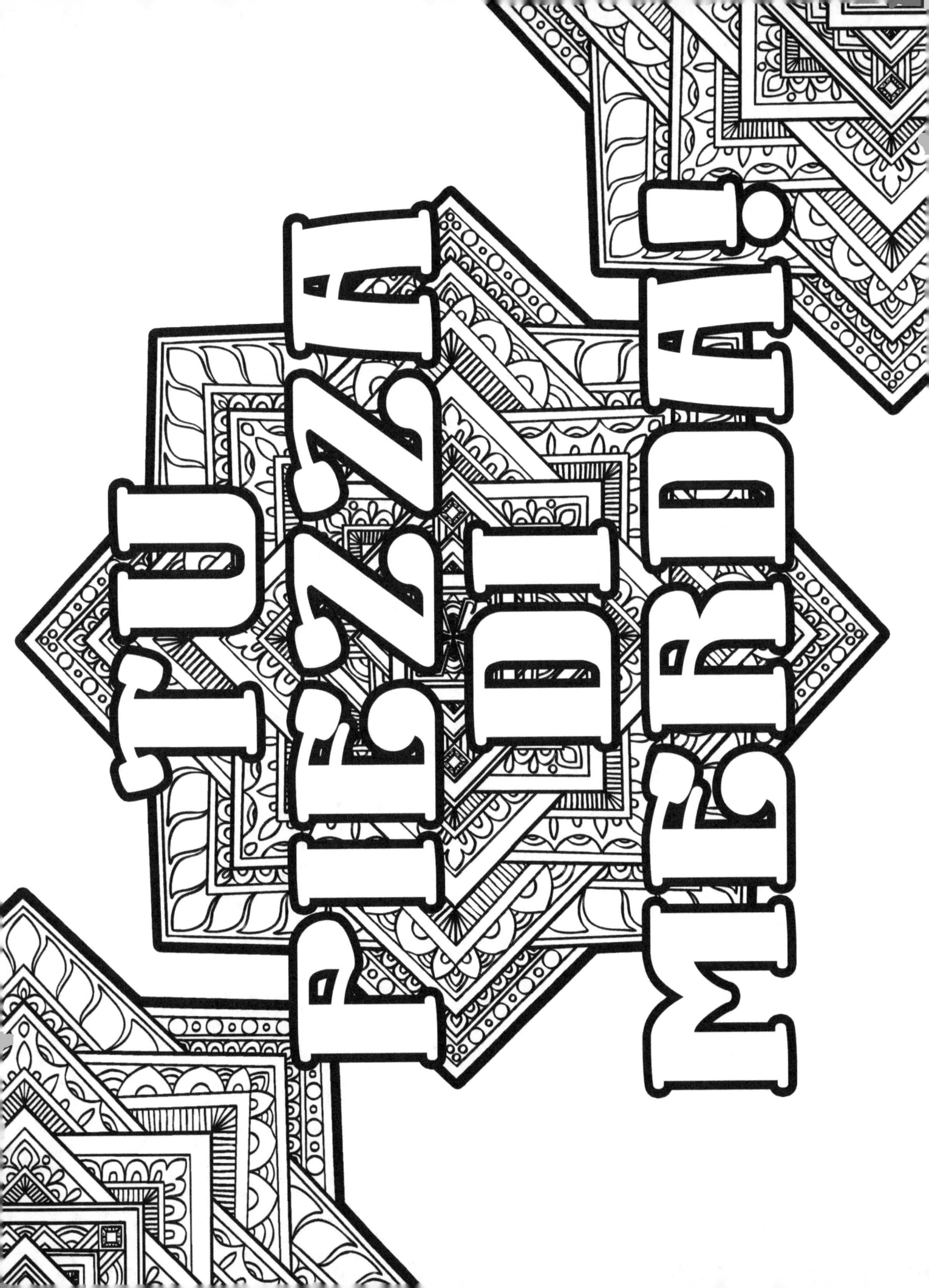

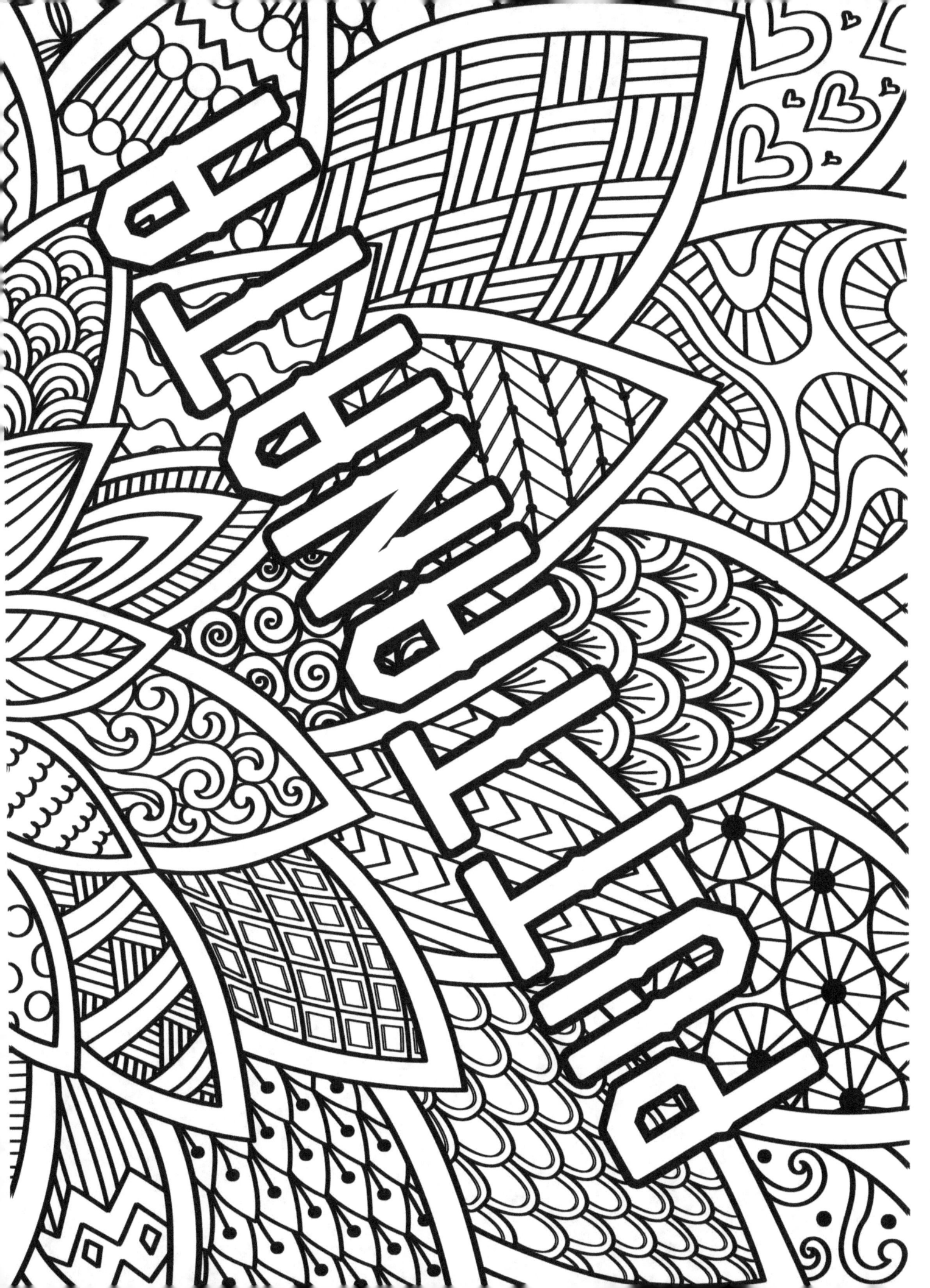

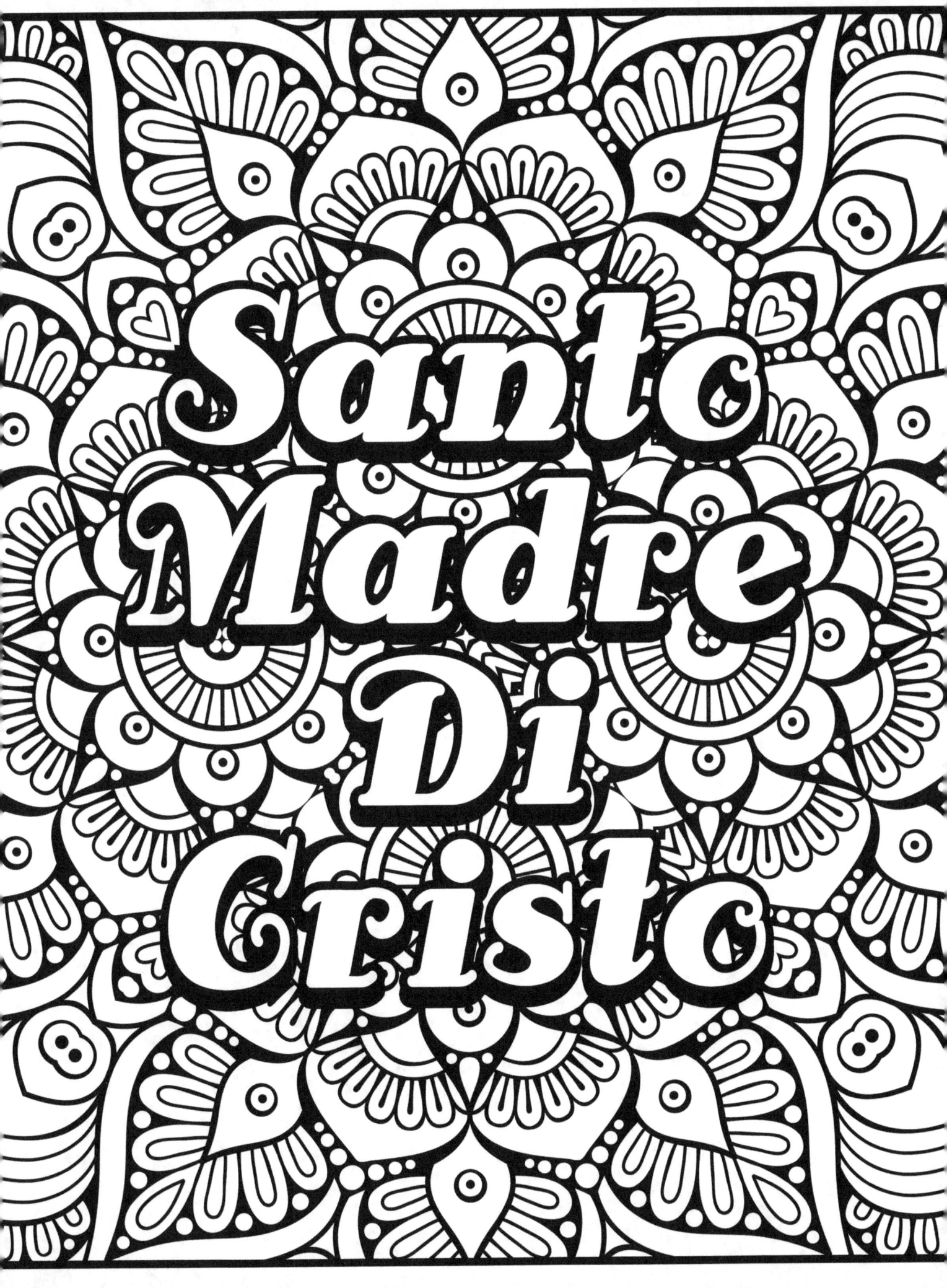

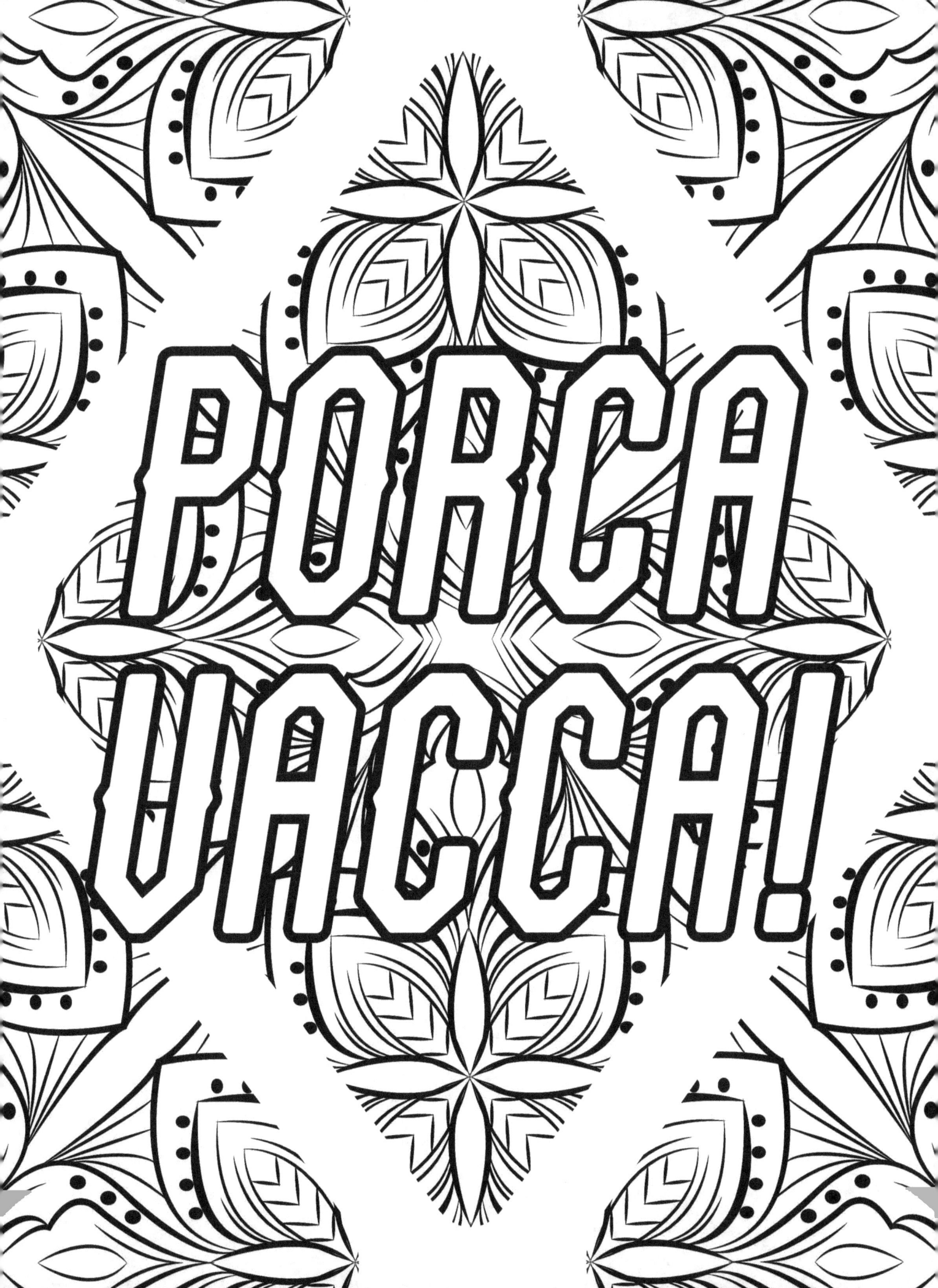

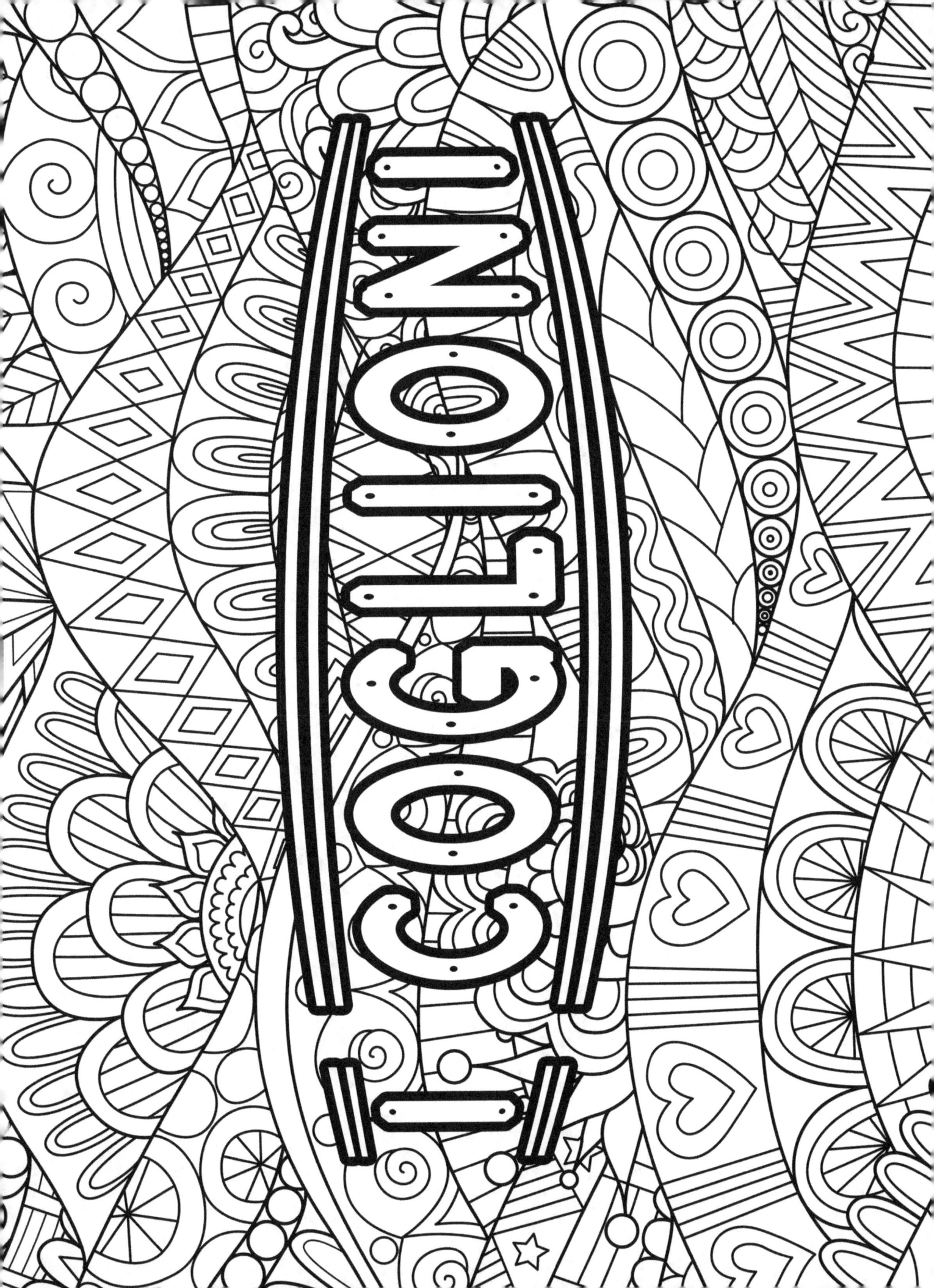

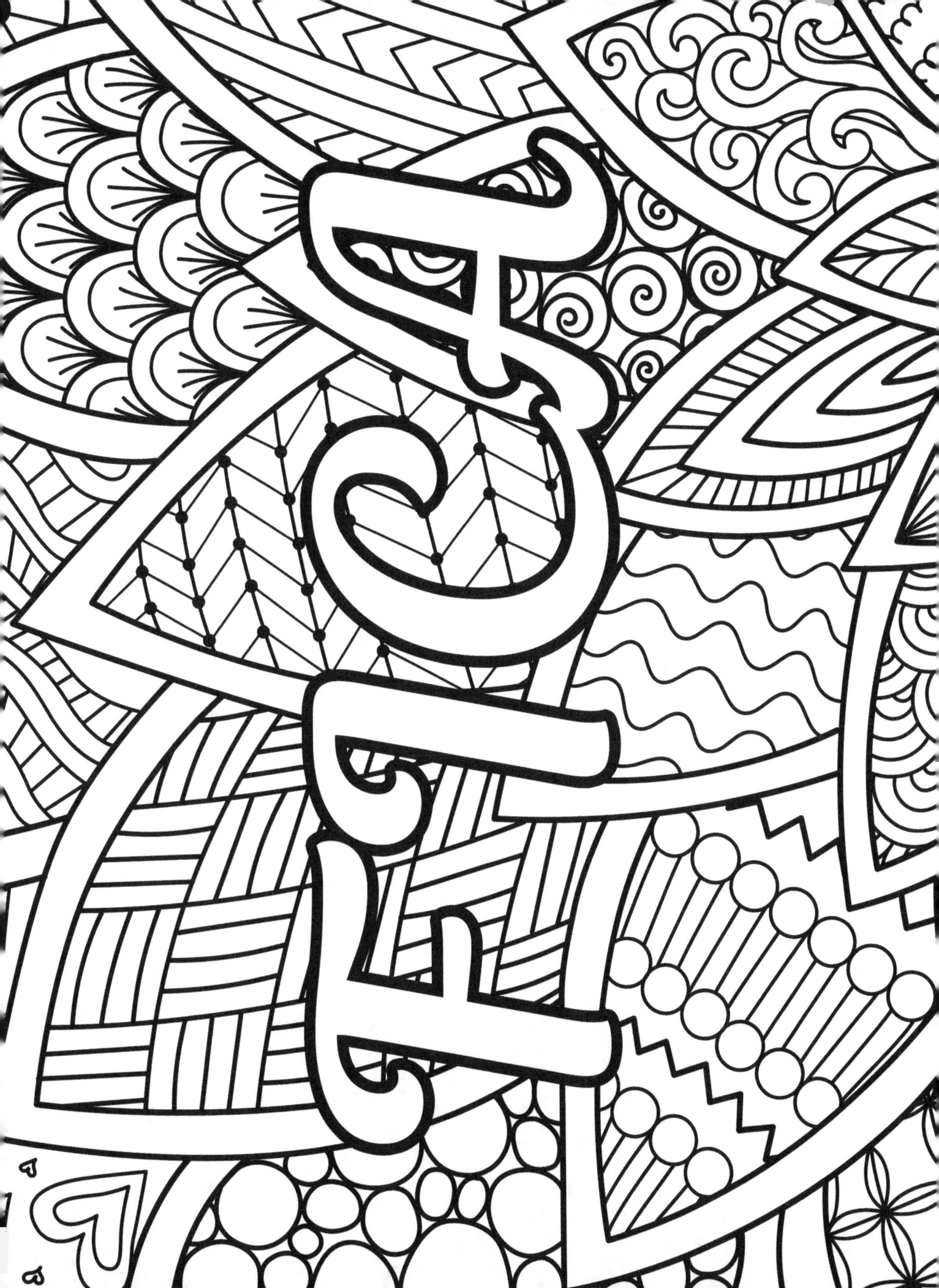

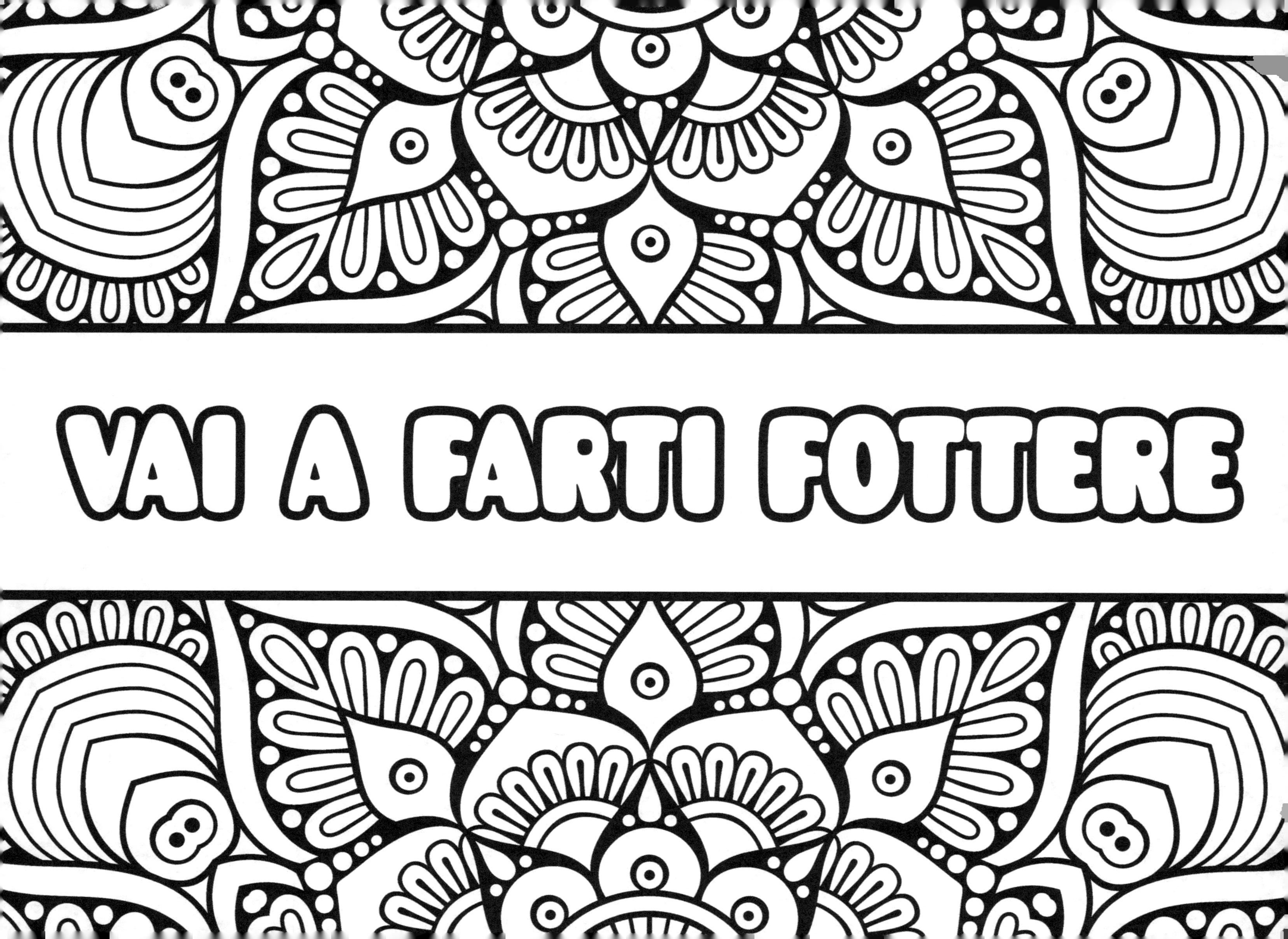

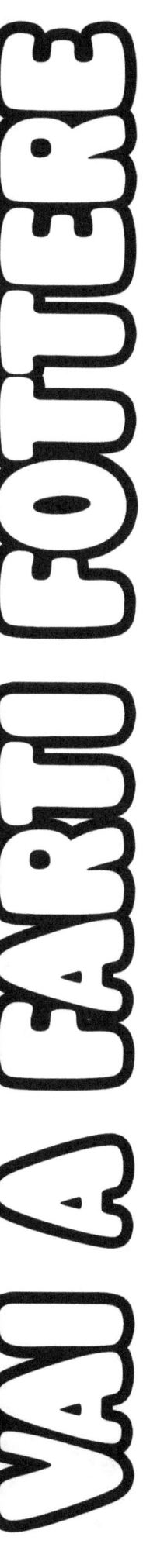
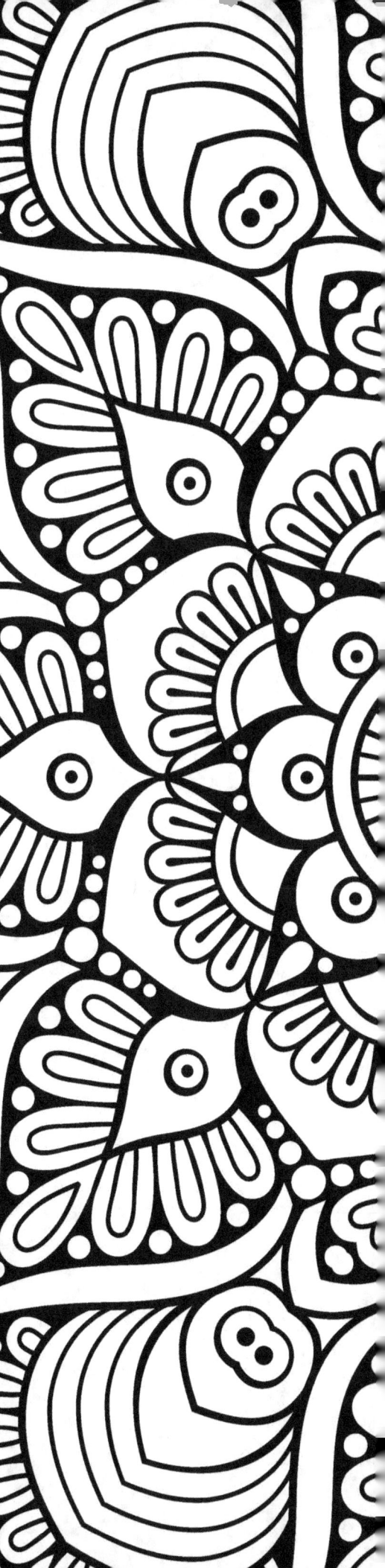

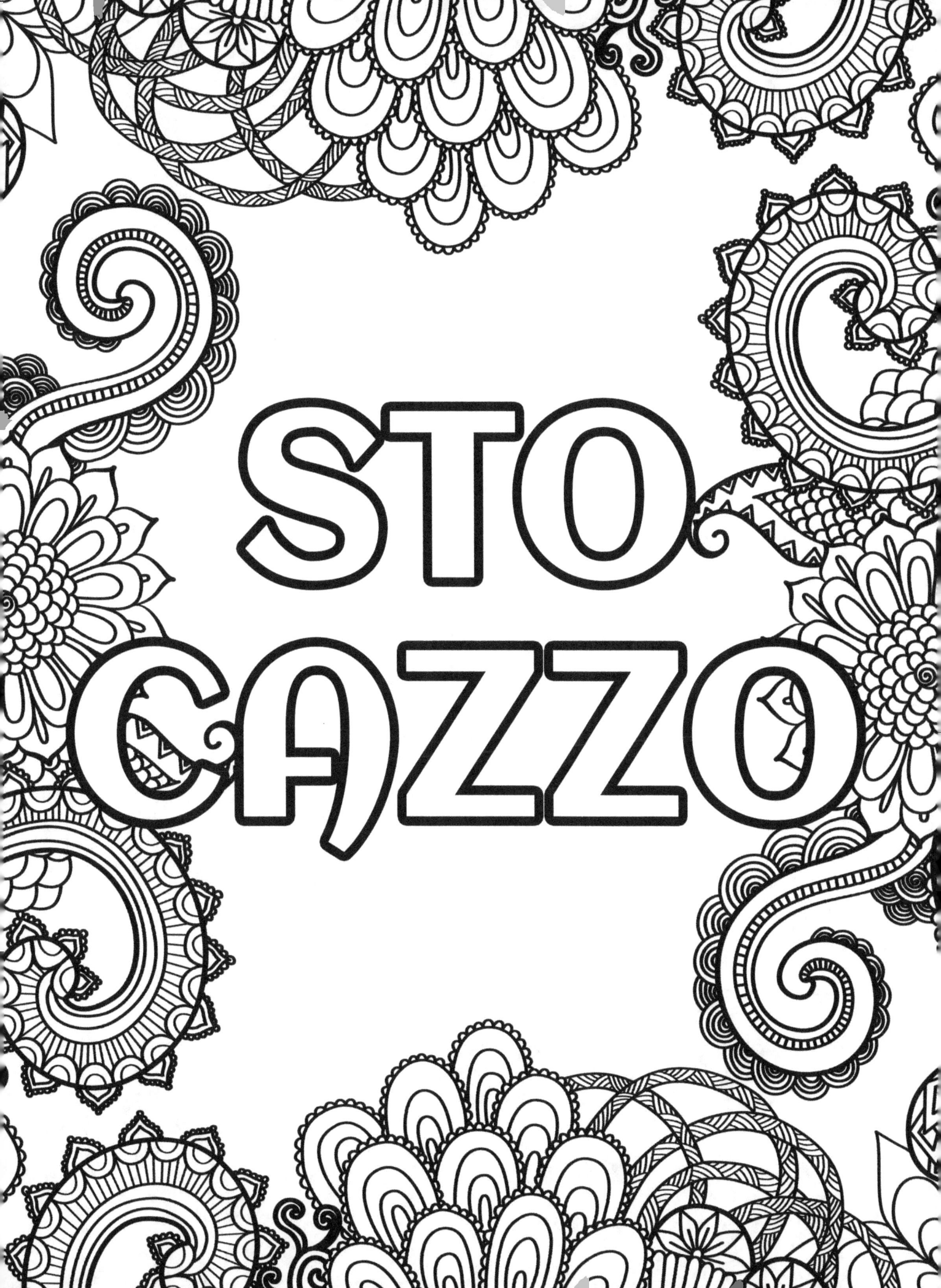

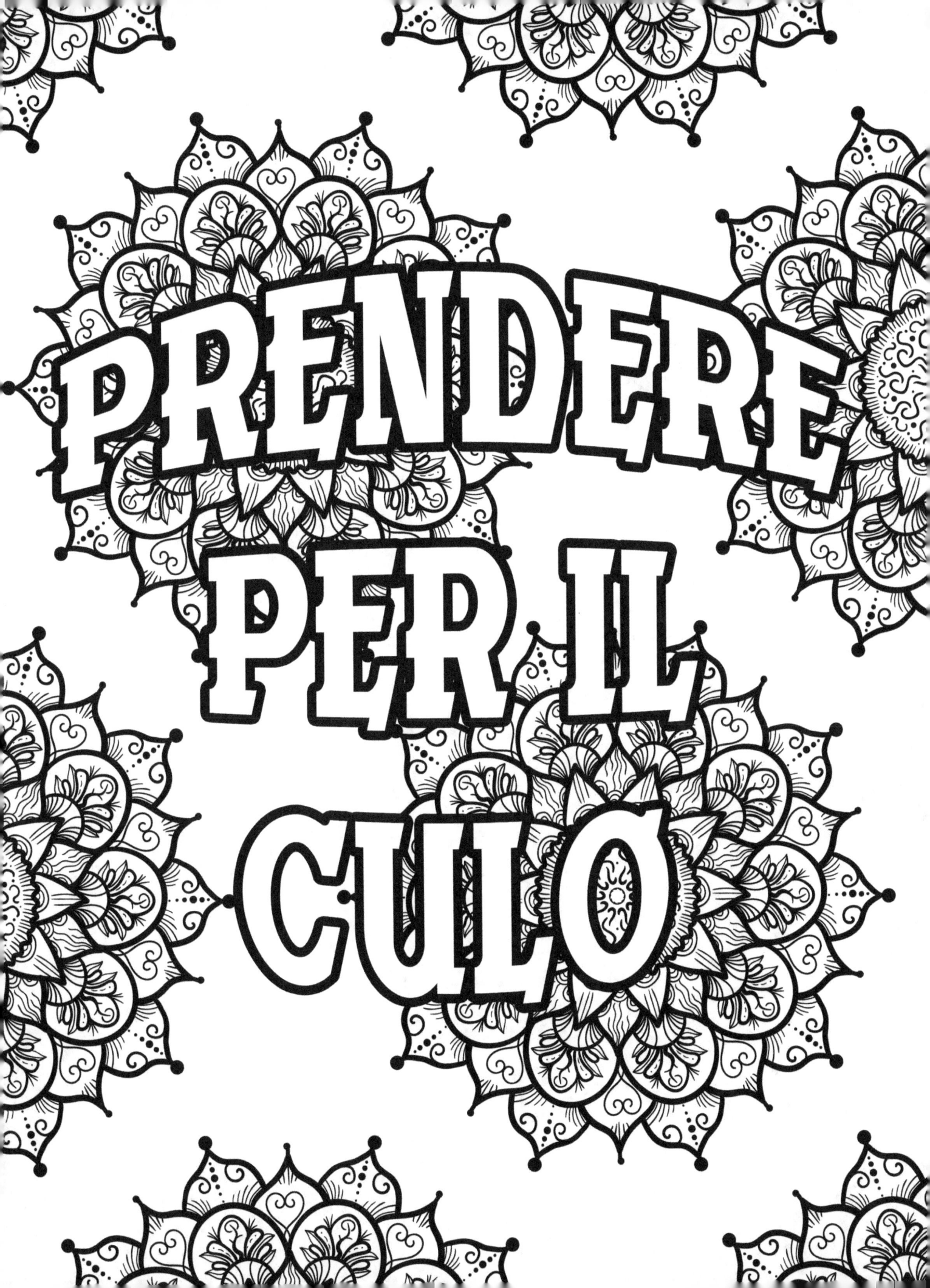

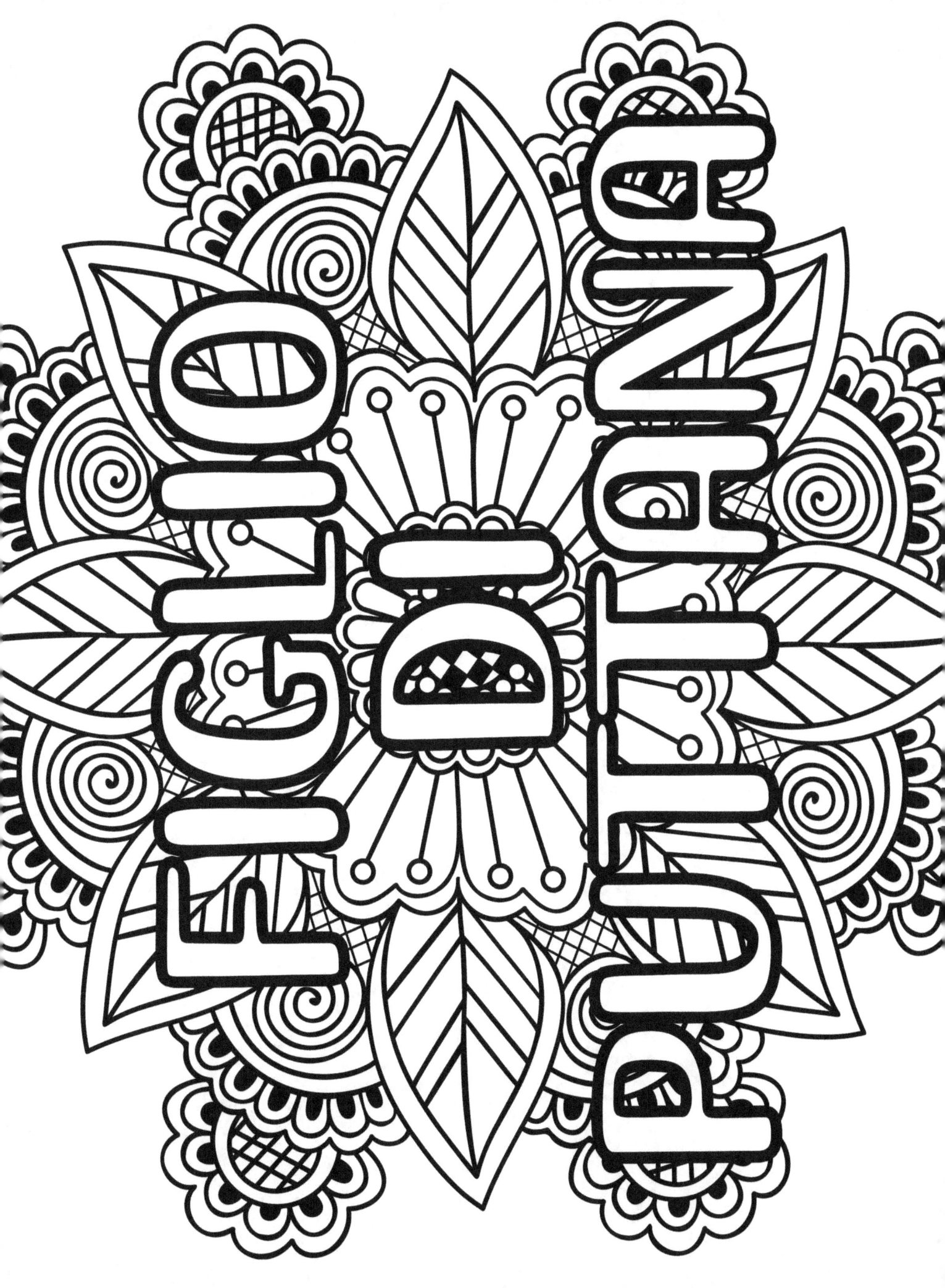

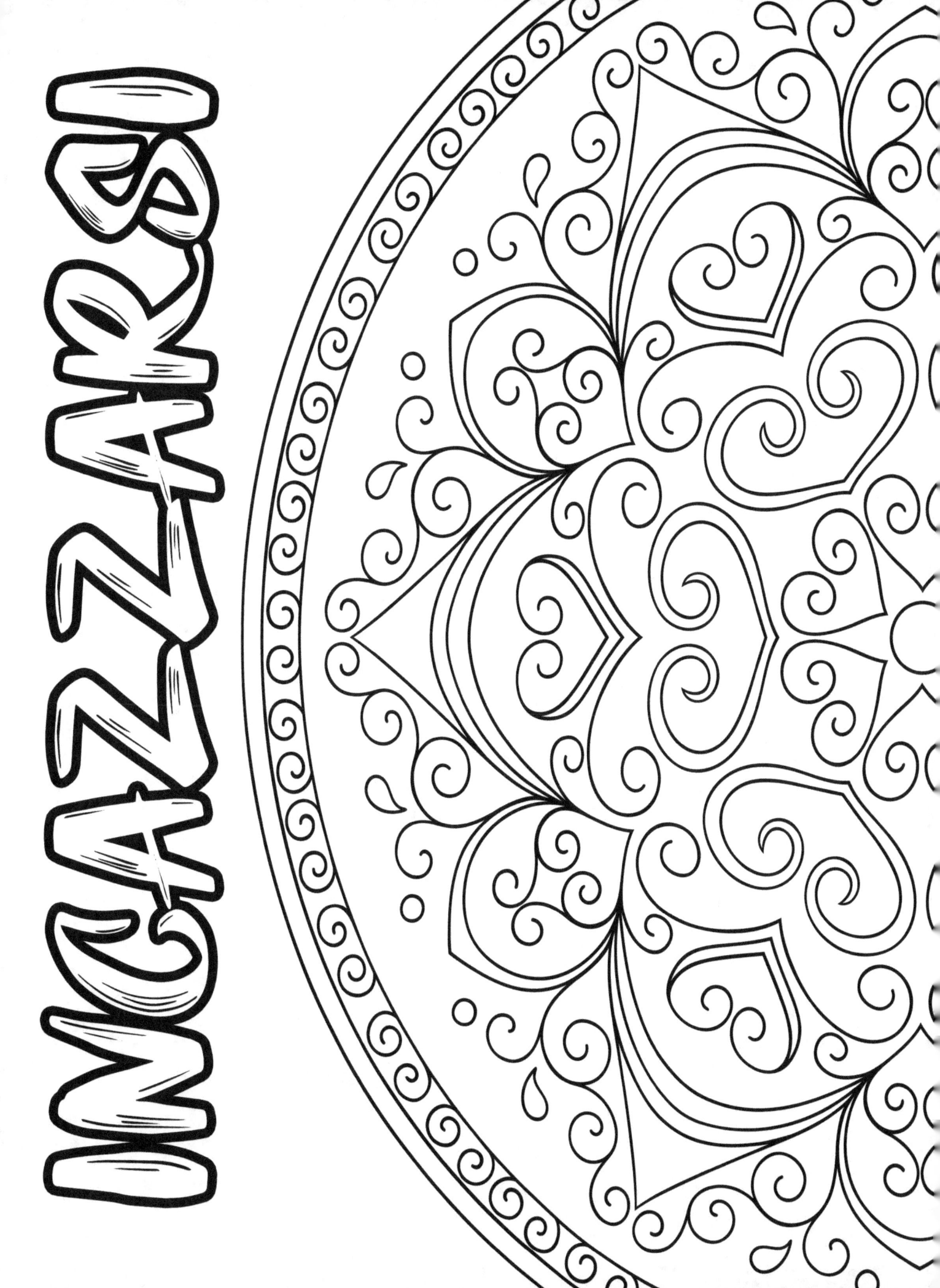

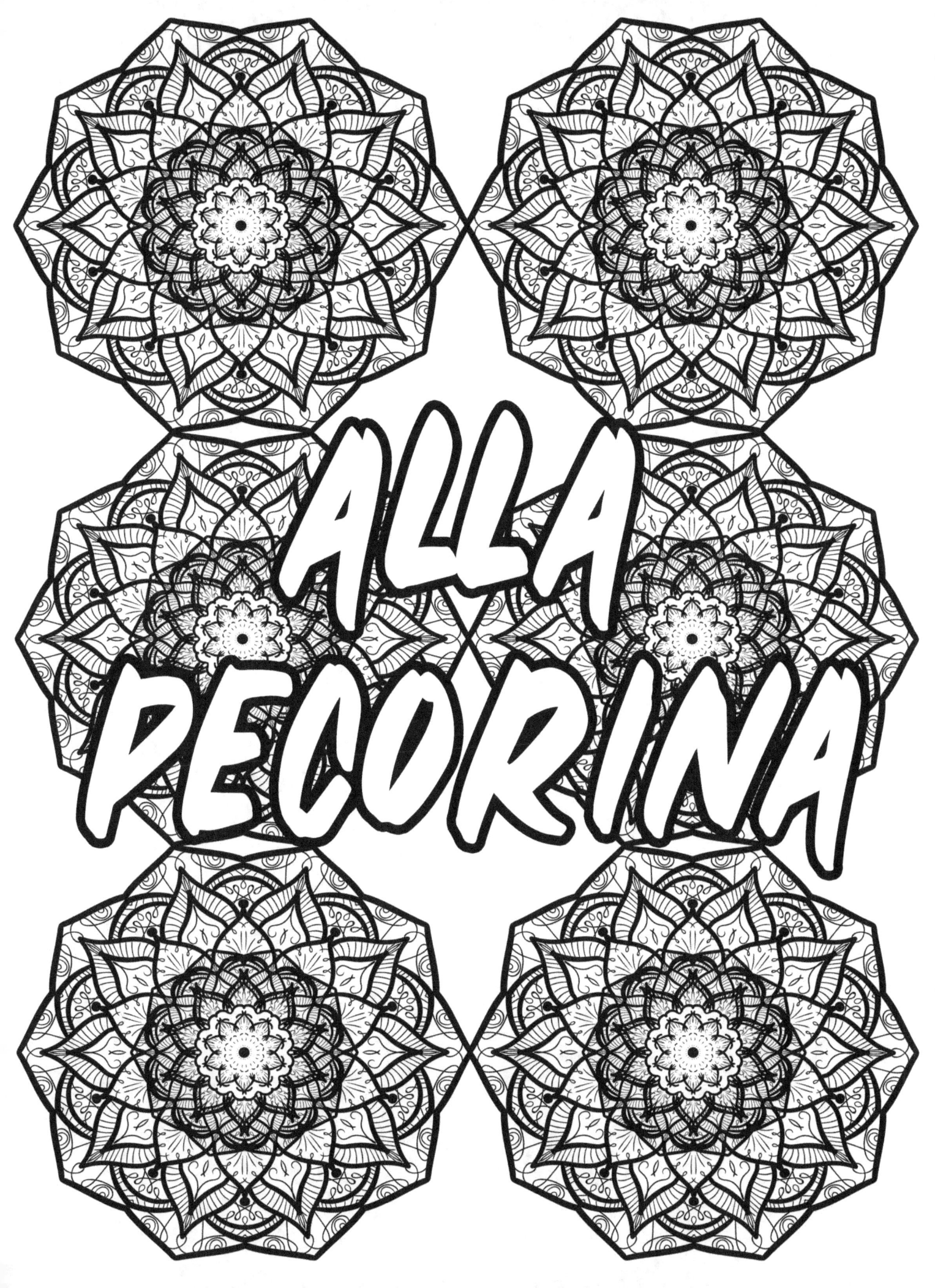

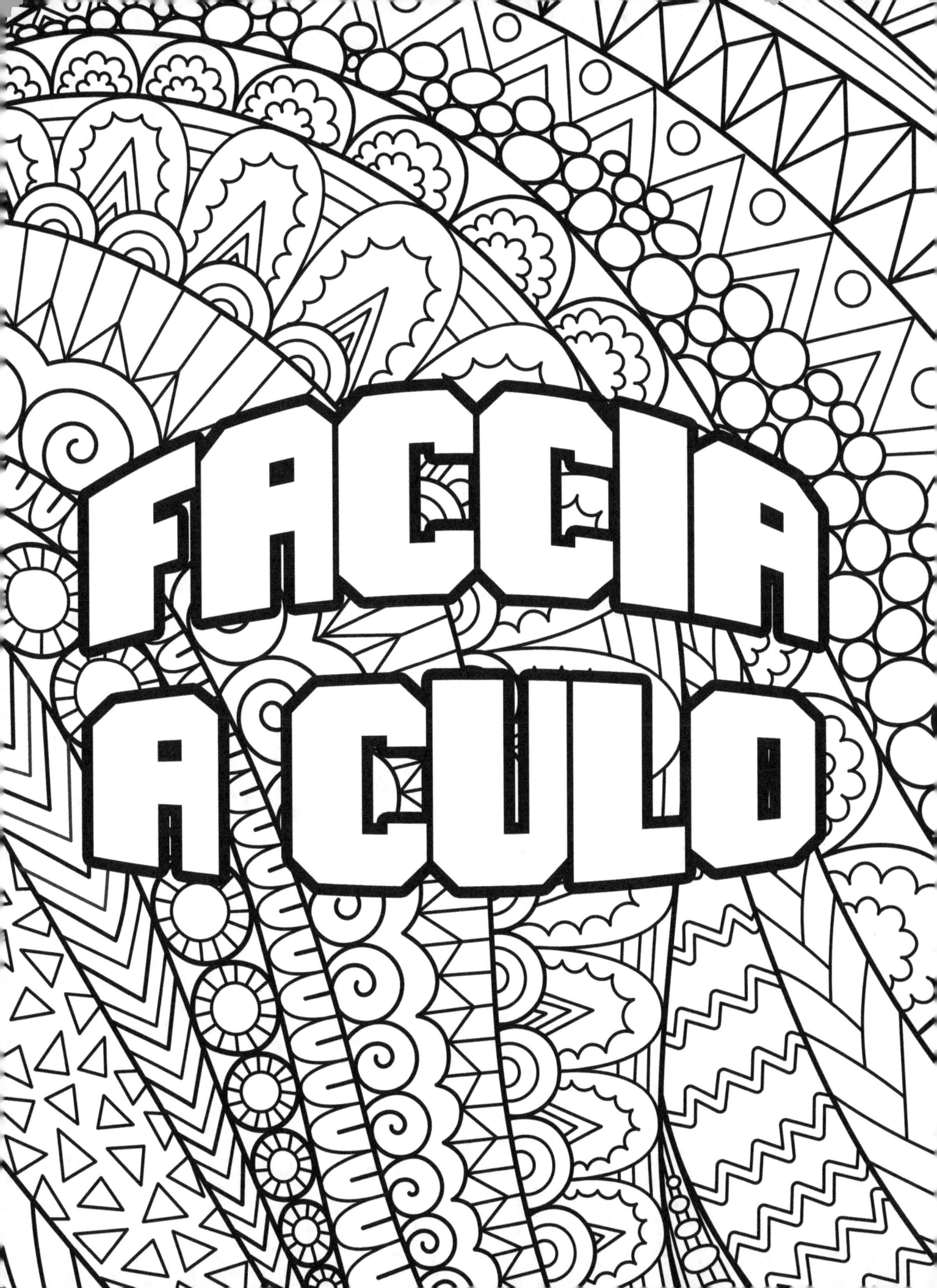

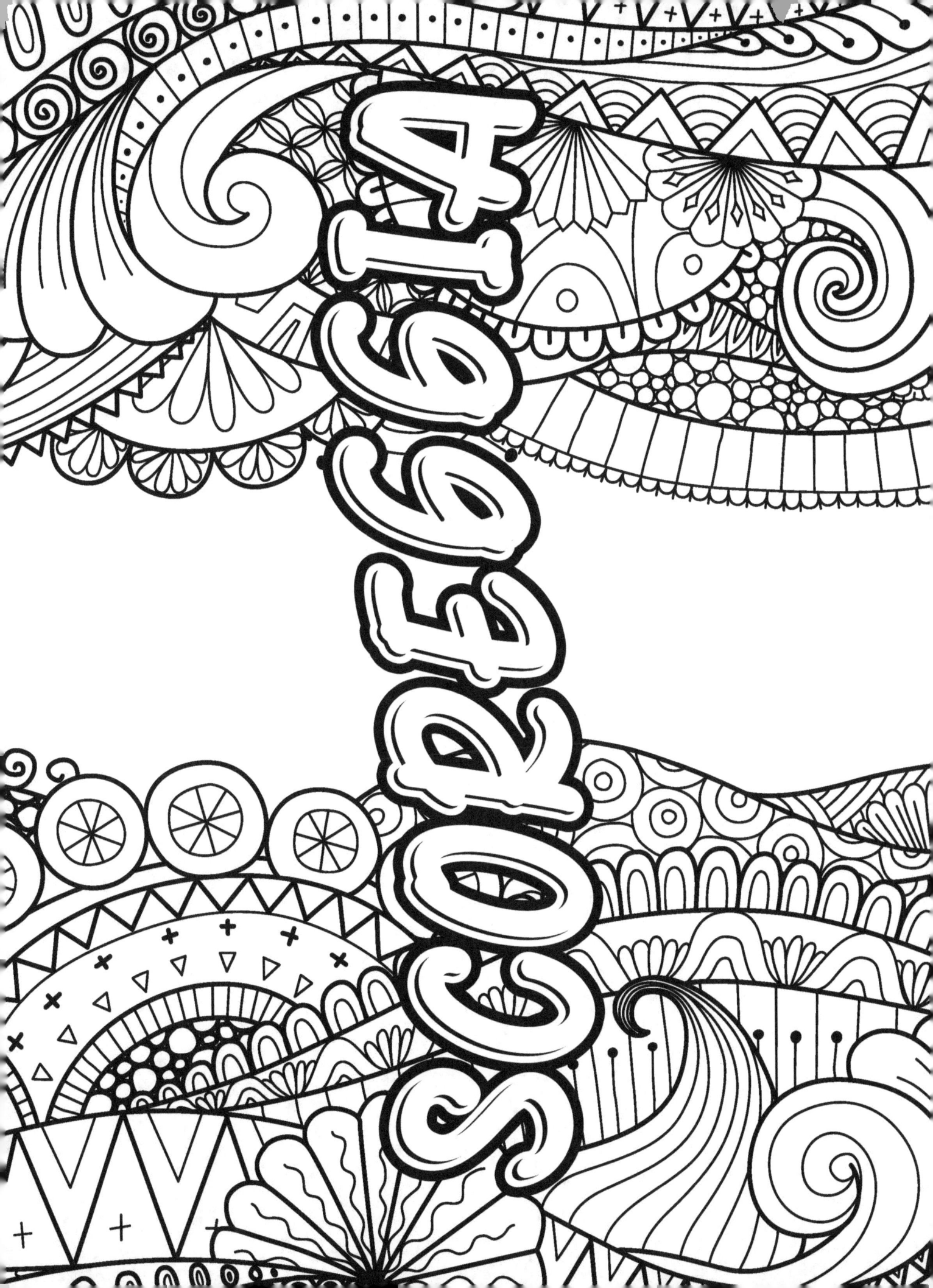

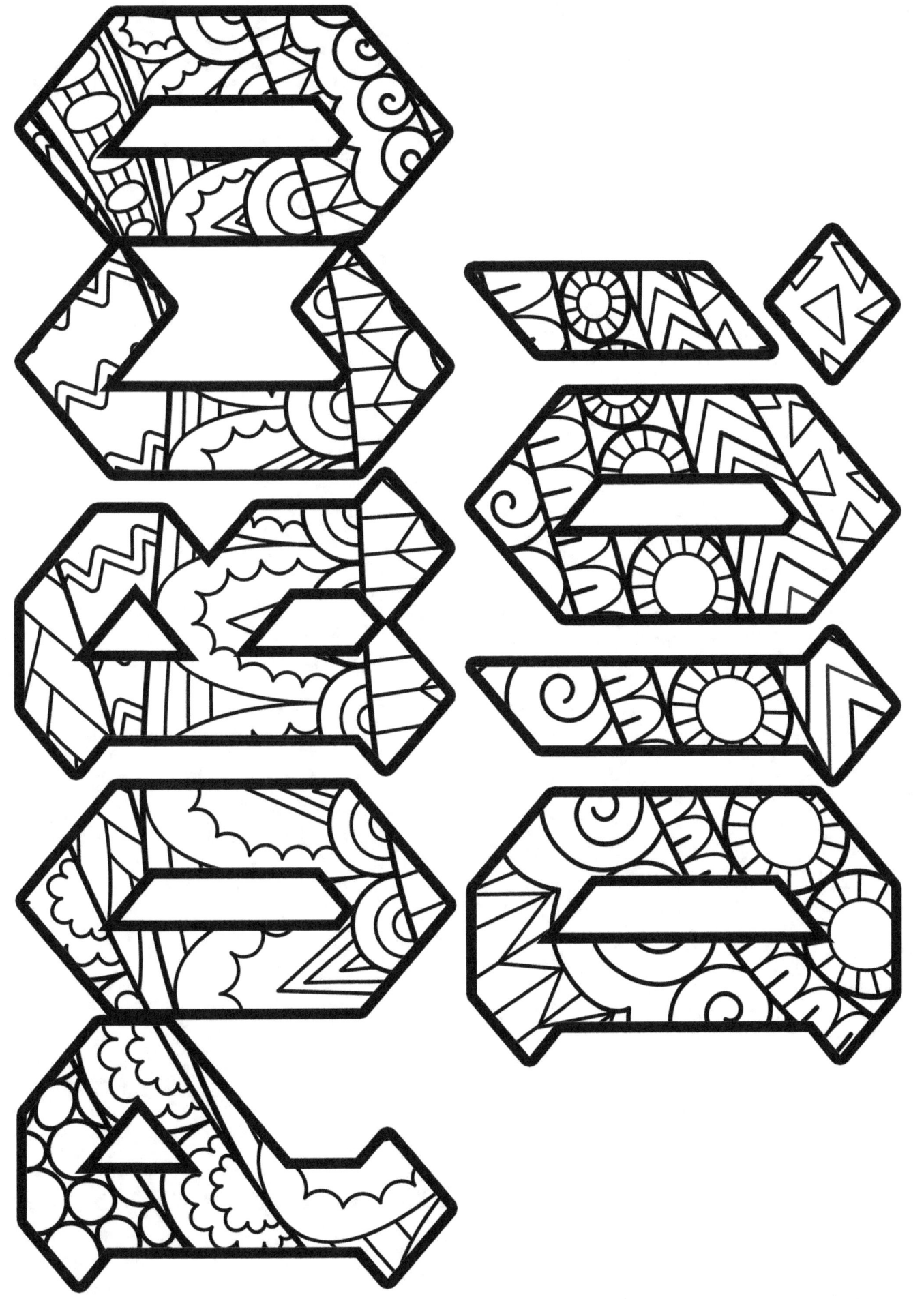

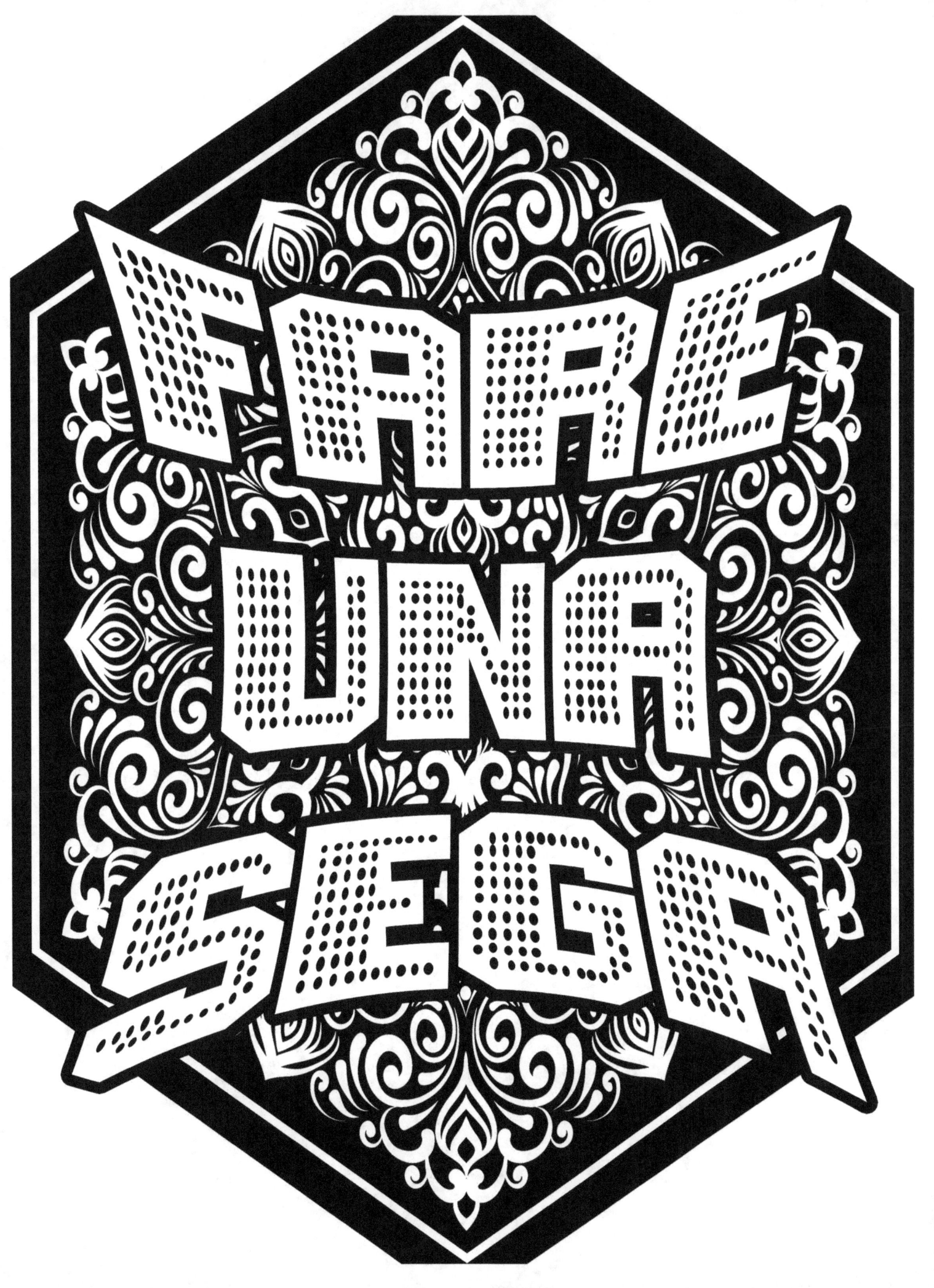

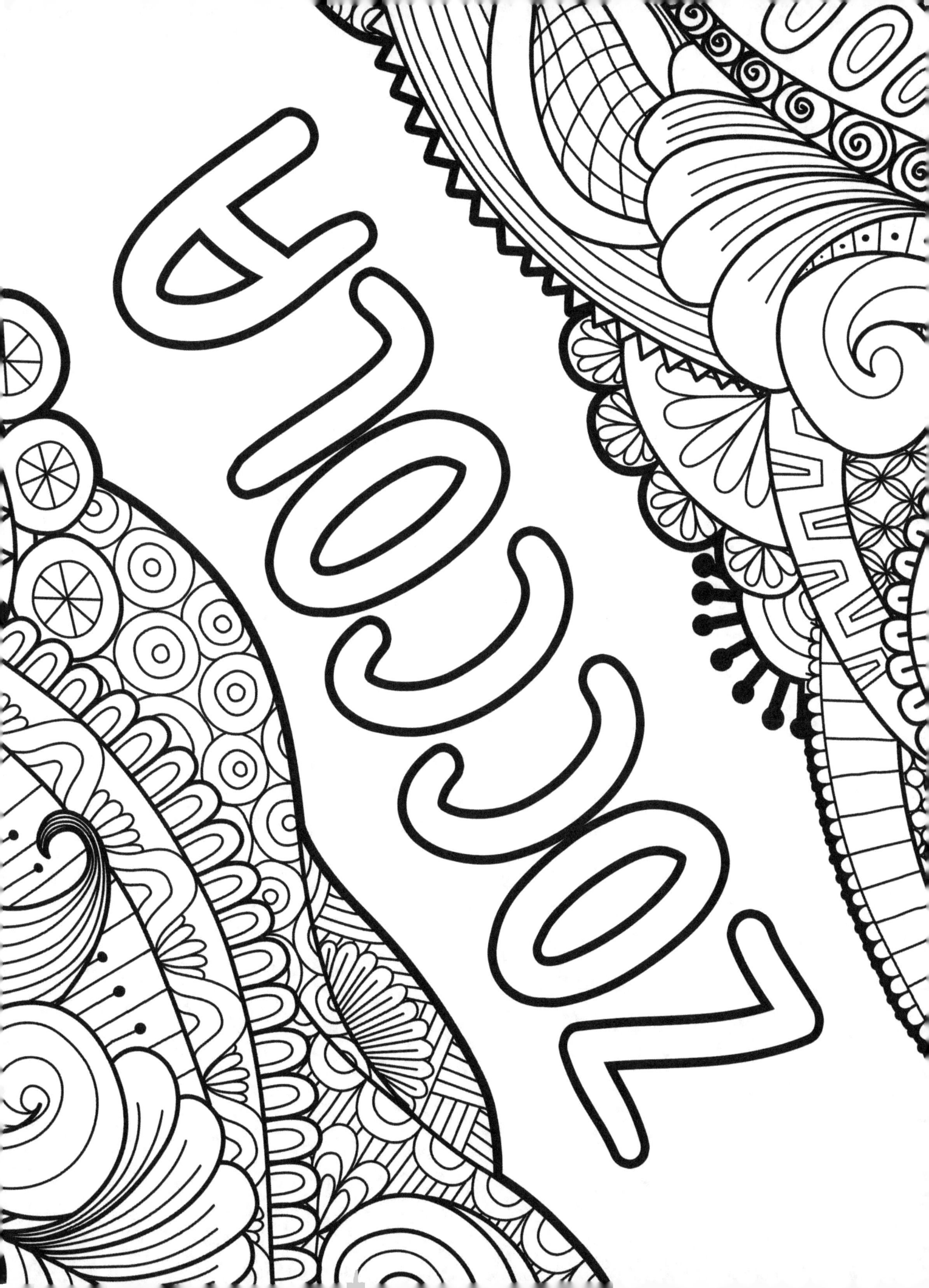

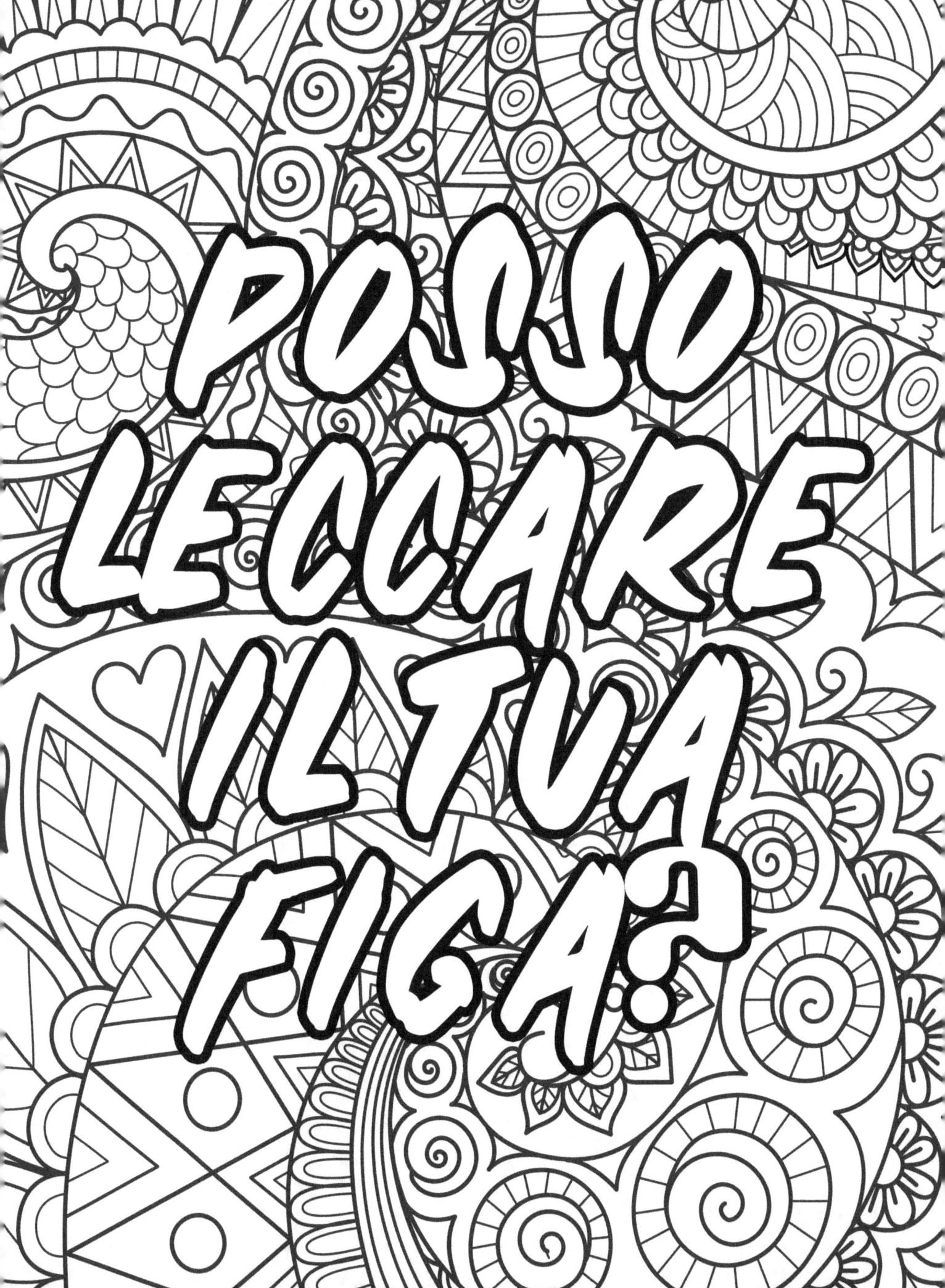

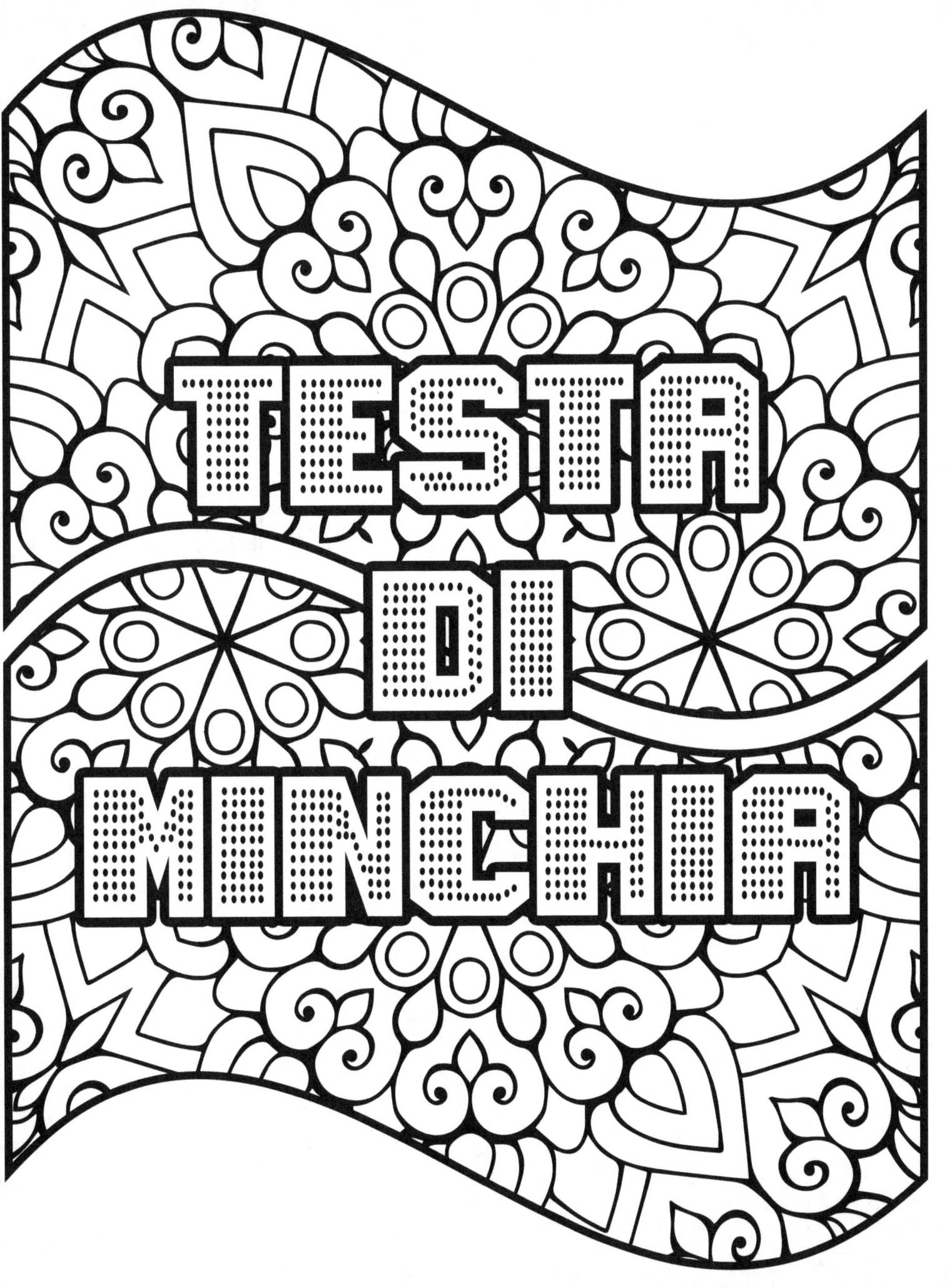

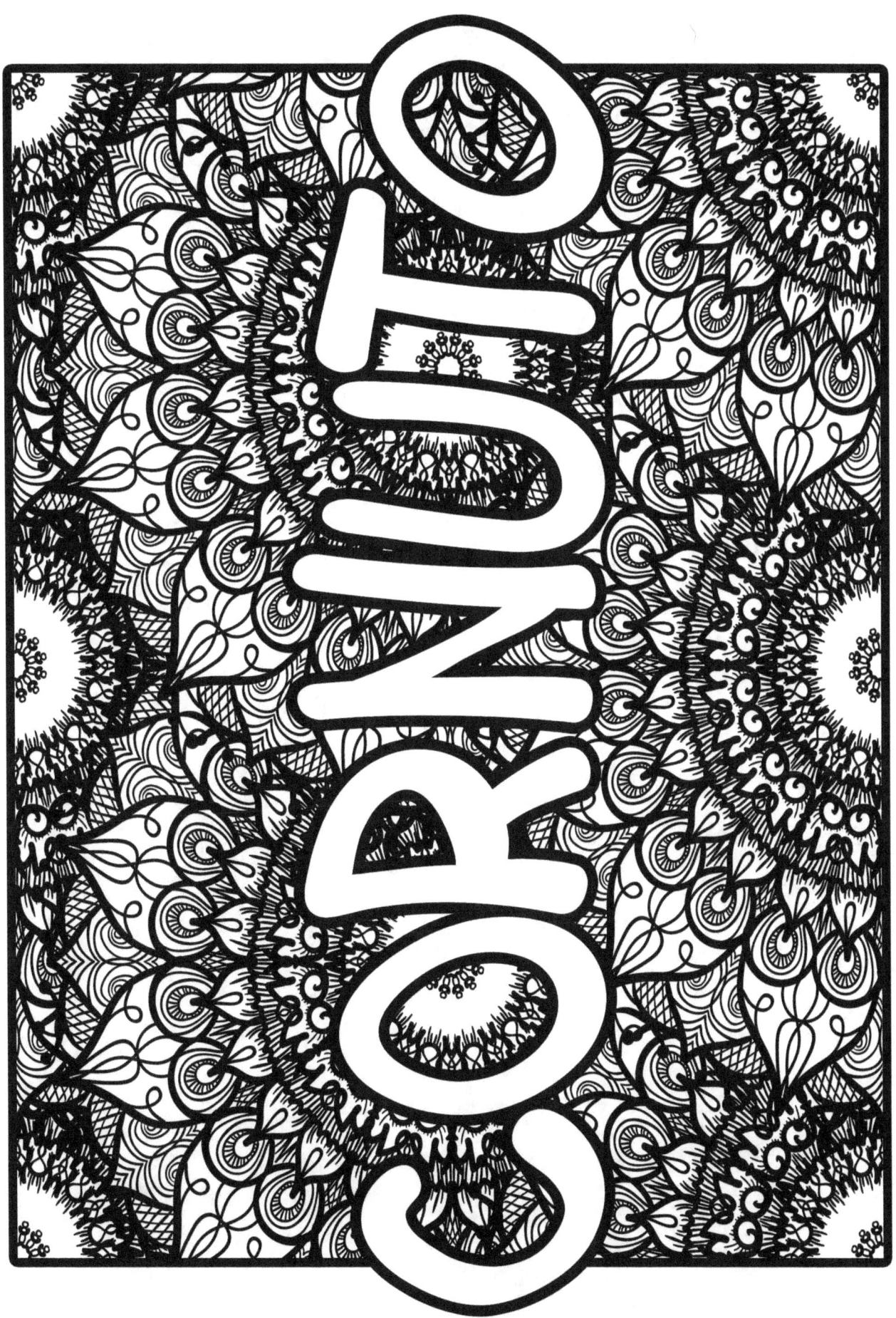

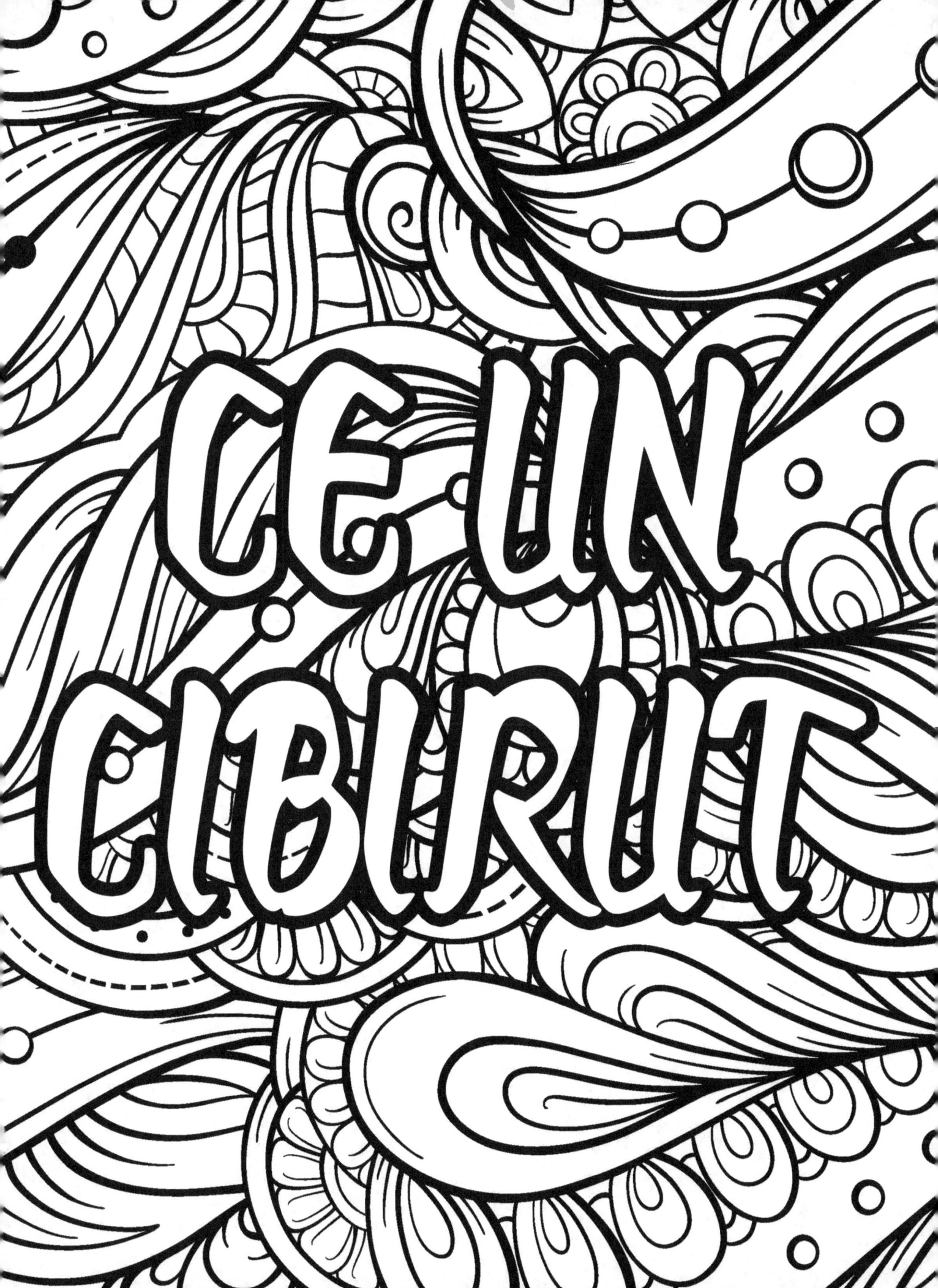

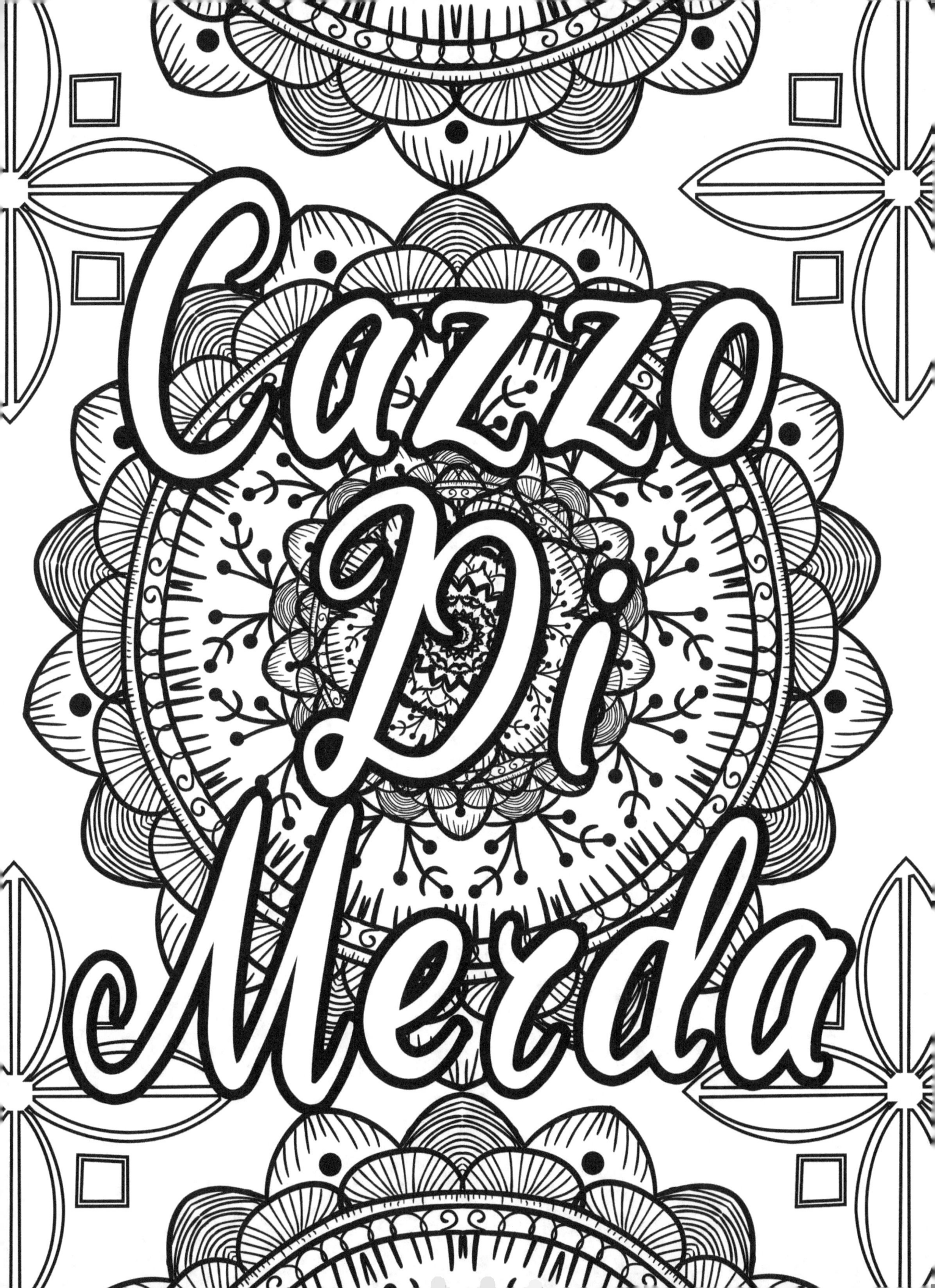

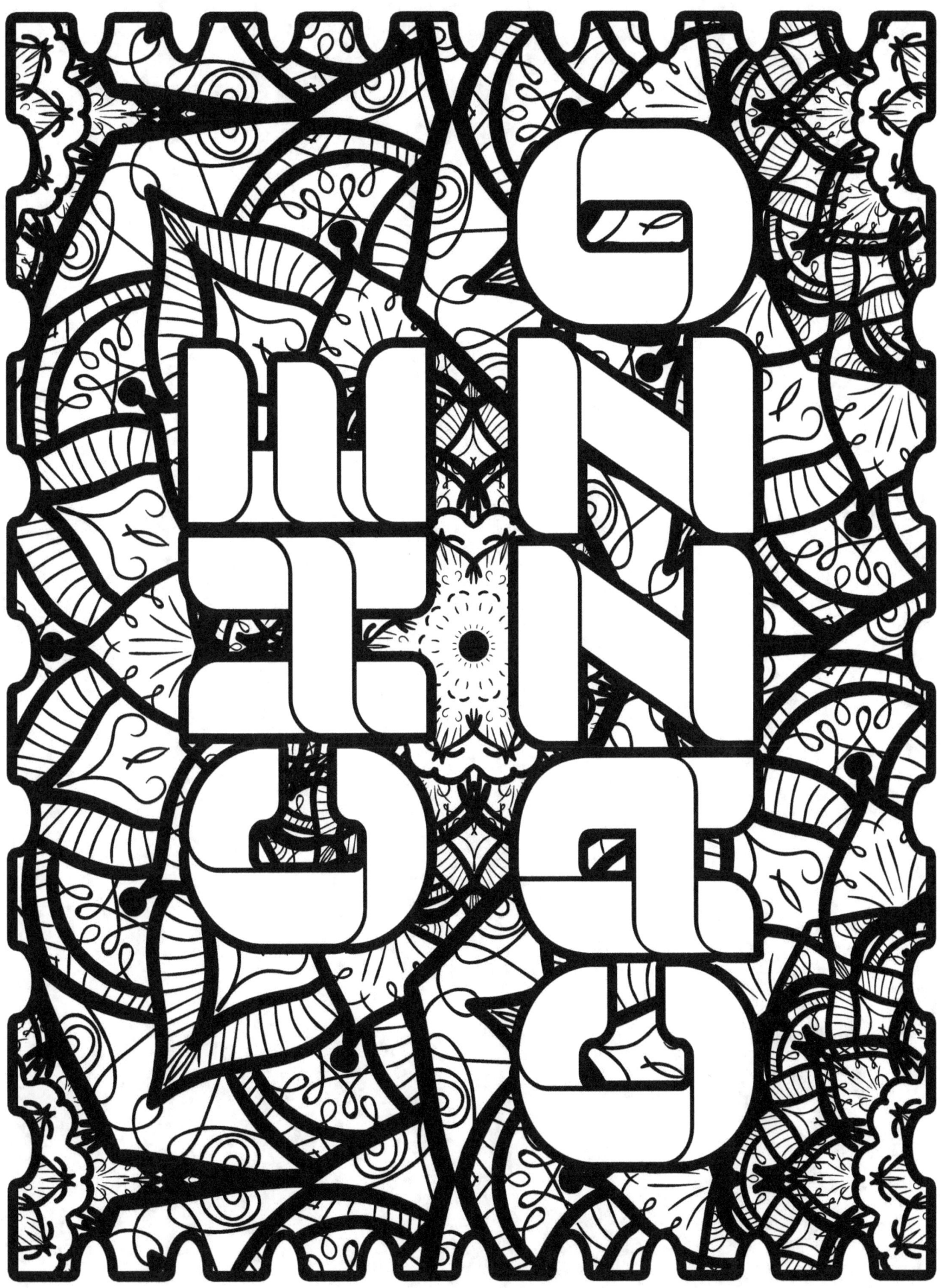

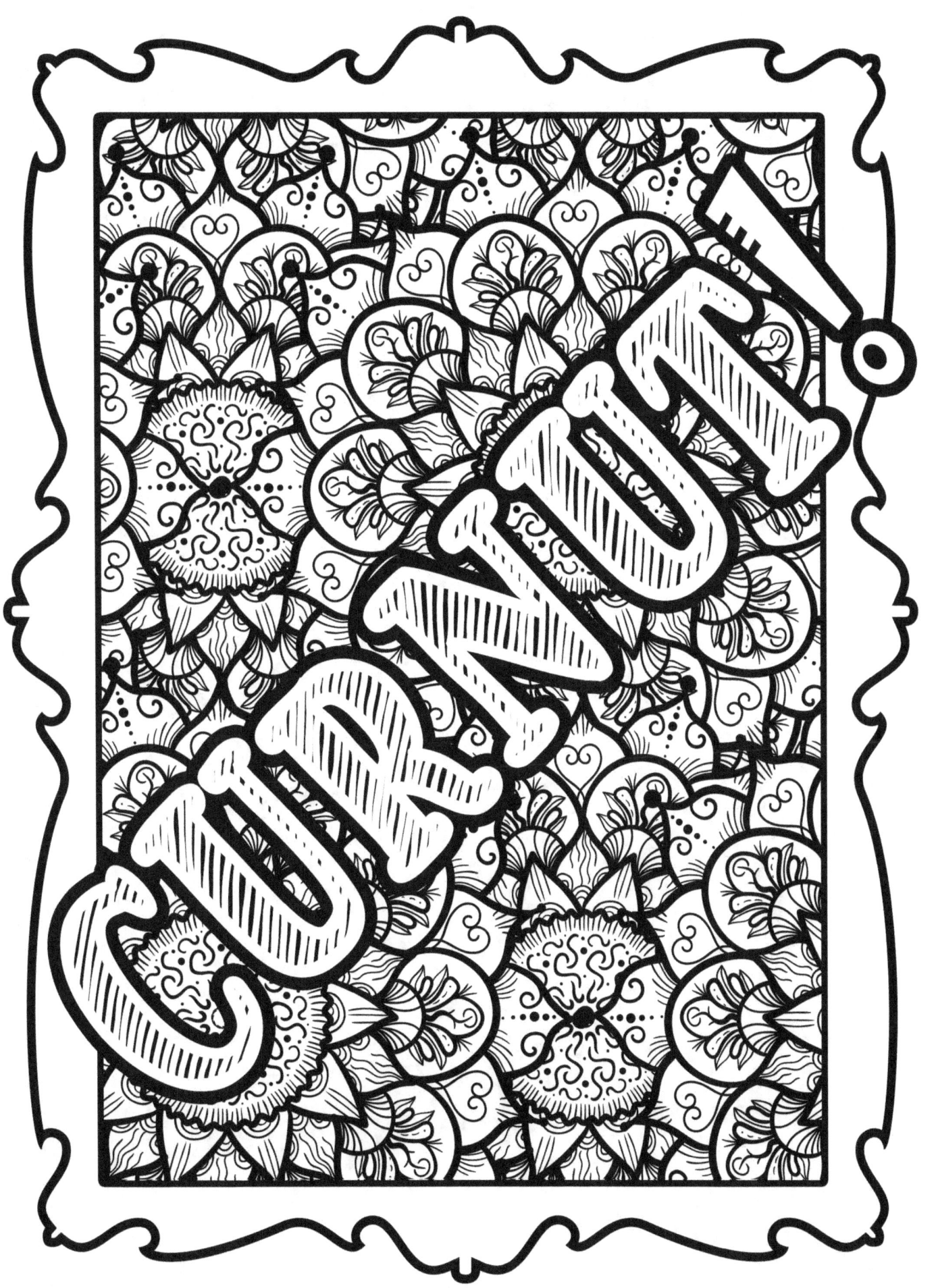

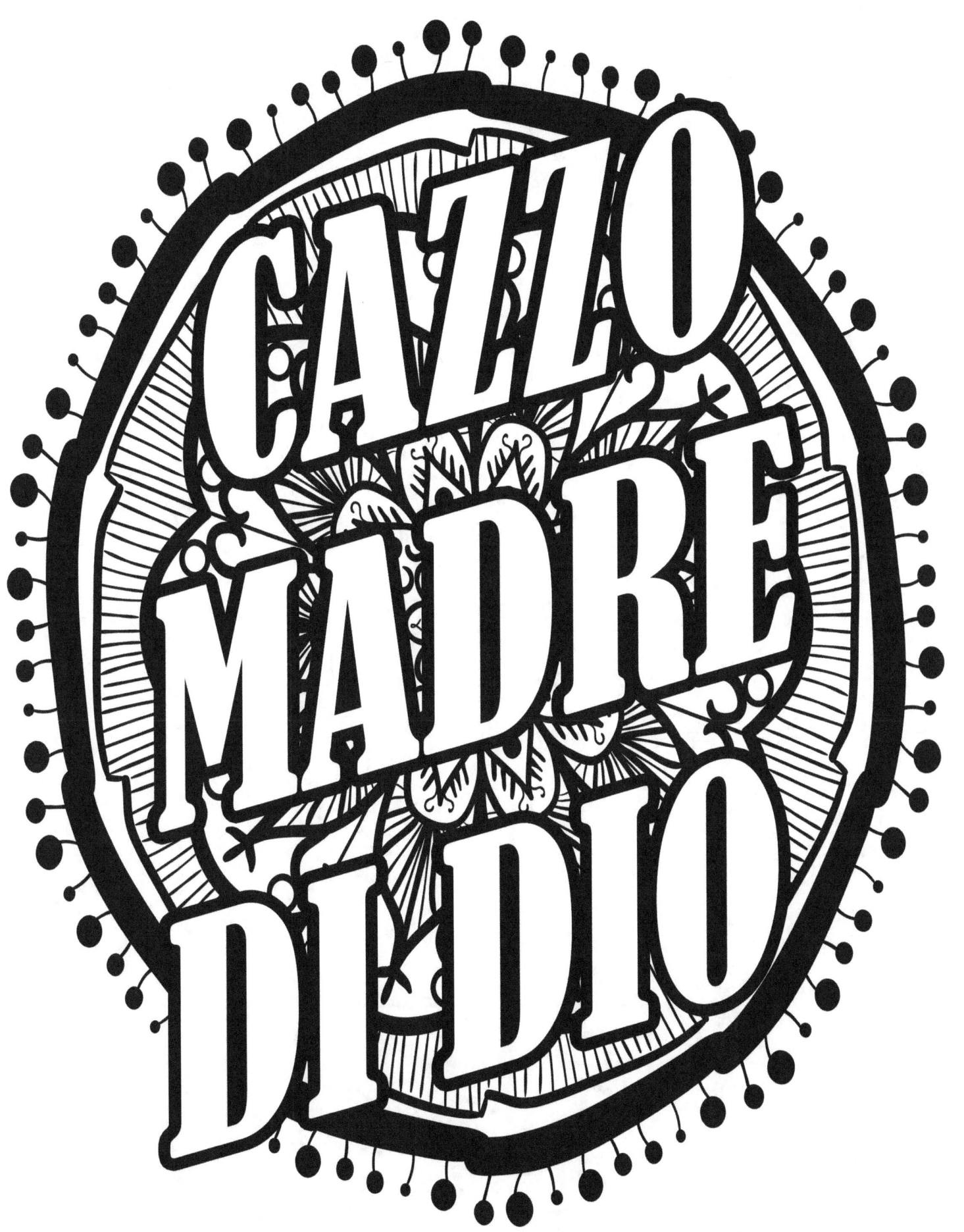

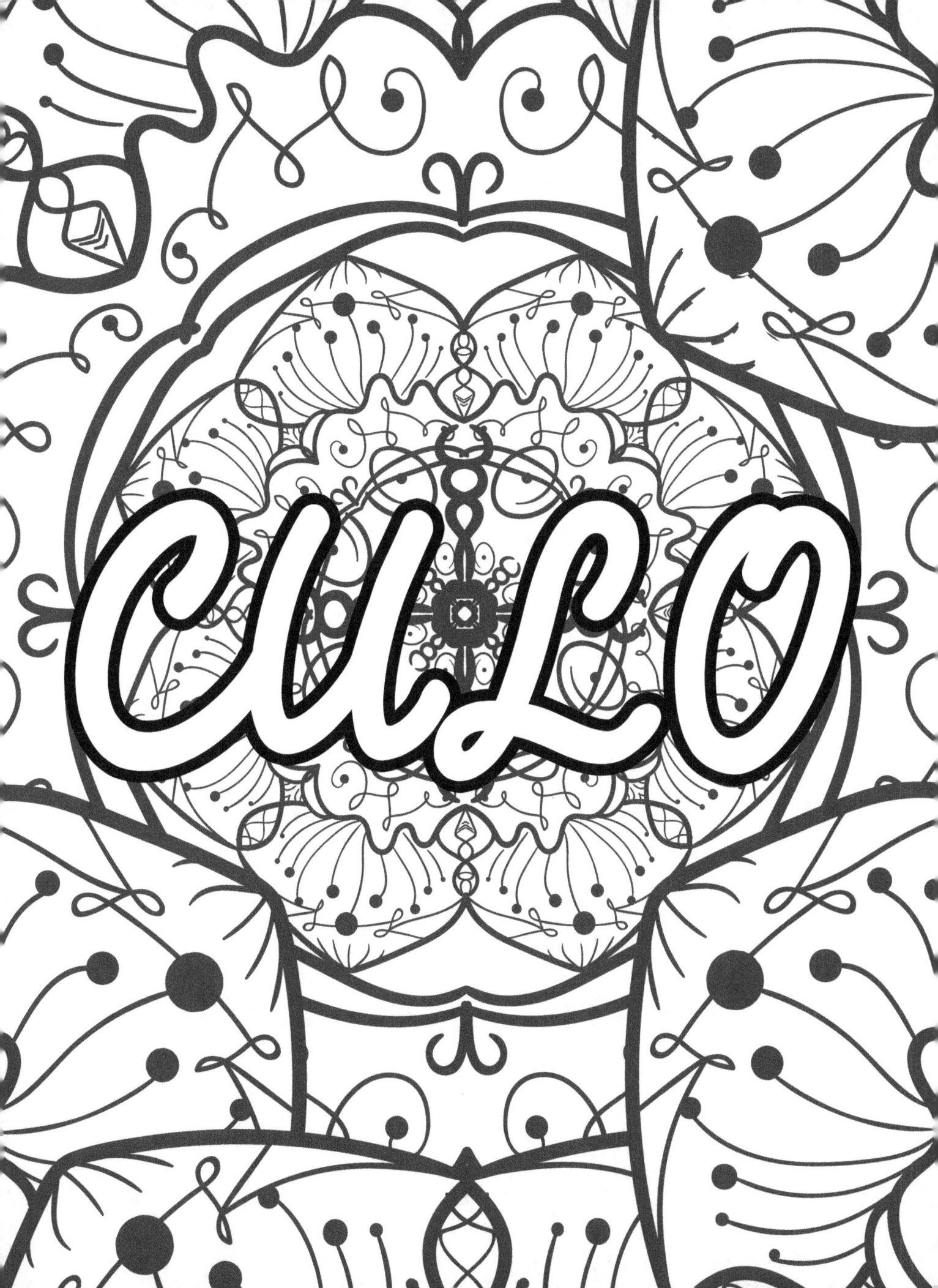

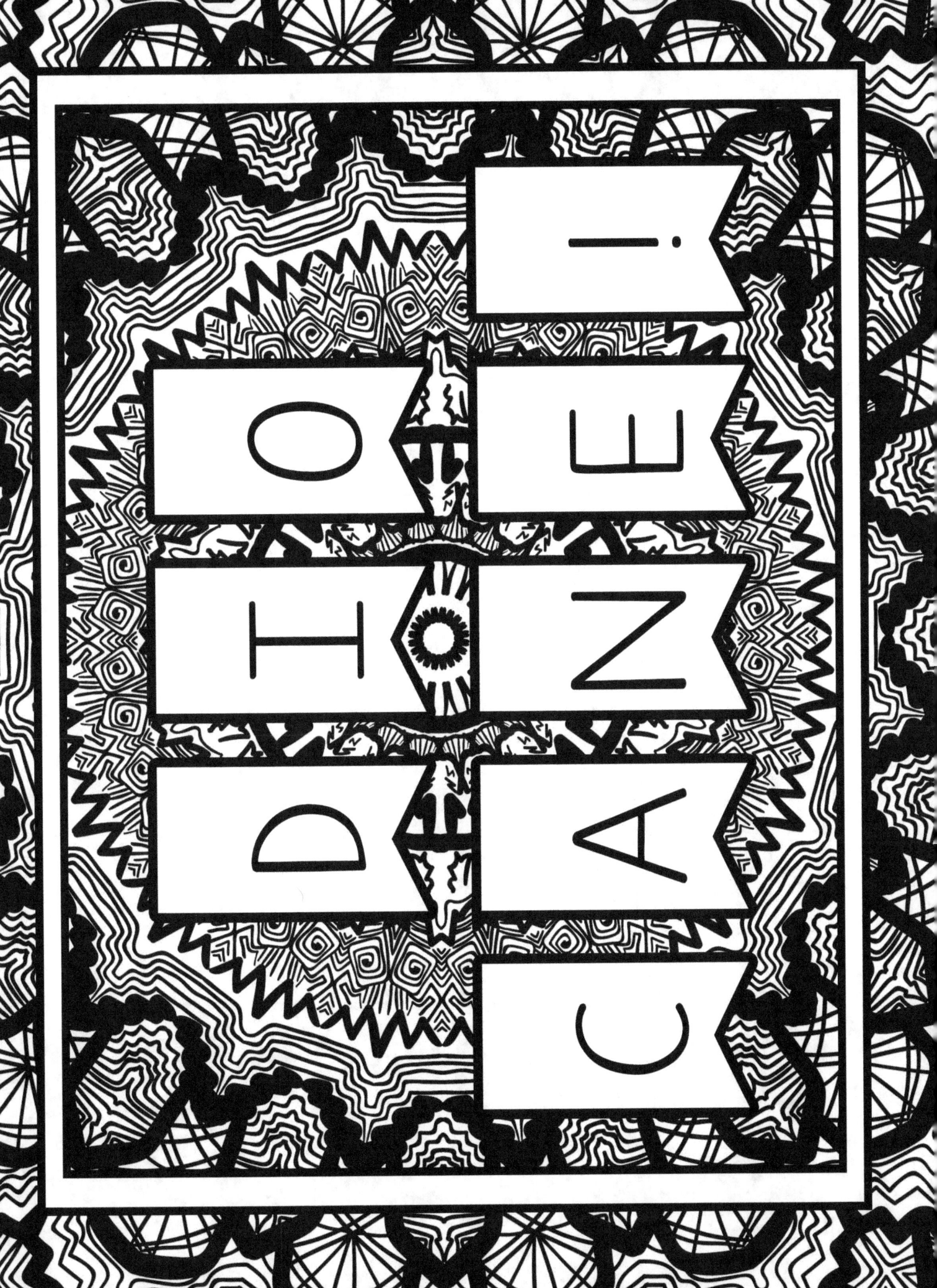

www.ingramcontent.com/pod-product-compliance
Lightning Source LLC
Chambersburg PA
CBHW080512220526
45465CB00006B/2459